SUCCESS WITH LIBRARY VOLUNTEERS

SUCCESS WITH LIBRARY VOLUNTEERS

Leslie E. Holt and Glen E. Holt

LIBRARIES UNLIMITED

AN IMPRINT OF ABC-CLIO, LLC
Santa Barbara, California • Denver, Colorado • Oxford, England

Library of Congress Cataloging-in-Publication Data

Holt, Leslie Edmonds.
  Success with library volunteers / Leslie E. Holt and Glen E. Holt.
    pages cm
  Includes bibliographical references and index.
    ISBN 978–1–61069–048–5 (pbk.) — ISBN 978–1–61069–049–2 (ebook) 1. Volunteer workers in libraries—United States. I. Holt, Glen E. II. Title.
  Z682.4.V64H65   2014
  023′.3—dc23   2013033814

ISBN: 978–1–61069–048–5
EISBN: 978–1–61069–049–2

18 17 16 15 14   1 2 3 4 5

This book is also available on the World Wide Web as an eBook.
Visit www.abc-clio.com for details.

Libraries Unlimited
An Imprint of ABC-CLIO, LLC

ABC-CLIO, LLC
130 Cremona Drive, P.O. Box 1911
Santa Barbara, California 93116-1911

This book is printed on acid-free paper (∞)

Manufactured in the United States of America

Contents

Illustrations

Introduction

This book will help library leaders who are starting or reforming their volunteer programs. At minimum, library volunteerism helps deliver the organization's essential reading and information services. At best, volunteers push or help carry libraries beyond improvement; they create the margin of excellence in different programs and services in all types of libraries. In some cases, the volunteer effort is so extensive and/or so effective that it not only aids in the delivery of library programs and services, but it grows the status of the whole institution with its immediate users and within its larger service community.

Written by two library practitioners, this volume addresses operational realities. That approach means recognizing the myriad differences among libraries, even those with similar demographics, incomes, and reasons for being. Varying types of libraries organize many different kinds of volunteer activities. In this book, this variety is illustrated with vignettes from many different, successful volunteer programs in special, school, university and public libraries—and from institutions large and small and those in between as well.

Many books and articles on volunteers have an evangelical quality. They suggest that a few simple changes will make your volunteer program exemplary. This book takes a different tact: It suggests that practitioners need to spend planning time and hold extensive consultations with staff to produce a successful volunteer program. Without such planning and consultation, a library's volunteerism is likely to become at best trivial and at worst a miasmatic swamp of discontent and complaints.

The overall keys to successful library volunteerism are relatively simple. Along with solid planning and effective staff consultation, it needs better staff/volunteer interaction rather than some stew of new organizational forms. It also needs fewer but a few well-recognized rules along with quality supervision, and regularly and simply measured benefits for volunteers and the community rather than vividly wordsmithed claims.

There are several books and some significant articles on library volunteerism. These are cited in the endnotes of each chapter. While we examined these books carefully, we tried hard not to pass the same way of our author predecessors.

Instead, an important feature of this book is its use of electronic sources. One of the great joys of working in libraries in the Internet age is how much of the national and even international literature that frames volunteerism is available on the Internet. The footnoting style used in this book makes every source, whether a broad concept, a quotation, or a specific example, accessible through a quick online search of websites.

That easy searchability allows this book's authors to produce a short volume, one not weighted down by forms available online or lengthy quotes from primary and secondary publications that users of this volume can quickly find on the Internet. Of course, the authors recognize that some websites—most notably that of the American Library Association—float through various alterations of electronic address, but during the time span in which this book will be used, a vast majority of sources cited should be available because, by and large, they are sources from well-established organizations and individual experts writing in their specialty knowledge areas.

To sum up, then, this book is relatively short and organized to be useful. It has an extensive table of contents and an index covering subjects, topics, and names of places and libraries mentioned or discussed throughout the book.

Each chapter stands independently, but their organization is a progression, starting with a brief rationale and context in Chapter 1. That chapter portrays volunteerism as a vibrant opportunity in your library and a rationale for this handbook for a successful library volunteer program. It reminds professionals that libraries of all kinds are built on a heritage at the core of which are voluntary users and supporters. Vibrant library volunteer programs make use of that grand heritage.

Chapter 2 is about hidden volunteers. These include elected and appointed advisory and governing board members, advocates, foundation members, and fund-raisers. In some libraries, staff act like this cadre of individuals are not members of the institutional voluntary community; yet they control policies and funding, and they decide how far to push the library's community and even their legislative agenda. Moreover, potential donors, elected officials, and civic leaders usually give greater credence to the voices of hidden volunteers rather than advocacy from paid staff members. Volunteers' credibility comes through their community and business connections.

Chapter 3 is about more traditional volunteers in library service. These include those who furnish transport, deliver books, undertake research, provide children's story time, and work in homework help—to mention only a few of the useful tasks that volunteers perform. This volunteer work in variant libraries is illustrated with many different examples.

Chapter 4 lays out the imperative process of planning new or reformed volunteer programs. It contends that library professionals need to do a good deal of planning —that is, thinking, conceptualizing, and strategizing—before loosing dozens or hundreds of volunteers on their library colleagues.

Chapter 5 goes a step further, suggesting the need for an implementation strategy featuring inclusion of present staff in the process and establishing communication mechanisms so that volunteerism is handled openly with staff members. A library volunteer program needs staff ownership and a solid implementation strategy. Proactive management is the way to gain that trust and support.

Chapter 6 is on recruitment, retention, and recognition. This chapter reflects the changing demographic shape of volunteerism. There is a good deal of emphasis on who potential volunteers are, the successful ways to contact them and to tell them the library's volunteer story, and appropriate venues in which to enlist their work in helping users of different ages with their reading, information, and community-building tasks.

Chapter 7 concerns volunteers in need of special attention. These include your Friends group, teens and other youth volunteers, disabled volunteers, and volunteers working for the library through partnerships with other institutions. None of these groups are exactly like other volunteer groups in your library. Working successfully with them, especially when they are allowed to take on quasi- or wholly independent assignments, requires clear connections and careful communication.

Chapter 8 suggests the importance of a Volunteer Management Information System. This chapter outlines a rationale for using an electronic system to manage volunteers even in smaller libraries because of accuracy and ease in communication. It also suggests how to set up requirements for stipulating what you want in a commercial system if your library decides to get a vendor to set up such an arrangement for your organization.

Chapter 9, like most final chapters in library-oriented monographs, states conclusions but within the context of where the information industry, the work world, and libraries are headed in the near future. Like the remainder of the chapters, it is the authors' hope that you will find substantial assistance here.

Finally, we provide an appendix that highlights an actual success model, an extensive and annotated set of documents that are the basis for one large public library's highly successful volunteer program. As most readers will know, the King County (Washington) Library System was *Library Journal*'s Library of the Year in 2011. KCLS is well funded and well led. Moreover, it is an institution that pays considerable attention to communicating with its multiple unions and its other non-union workers as well. This chapter contains multiple documents, each of them a working policy statement within KCLS. Every document in this collection contains the authors' analysis of why this whole document or a particular section of a document is written in the way it is. In other words, no document is presented "raw." Instead, all are reproduced with an analysis of their policy or procedural intent.

As you can see from this introduction, this book's authors have attempted to help library practitioners plan and implement a successful library volunteer program. To carry forward an ideal put forth by Daniel Boorstin, a former head of the Smithsonian and a former Librarian of Congress, the most-used books in every literate society are those that get worn out. In that vein, the authors of this book wish you fruitful reading. It is hoped that you and your colleagues will find this book so useful that you will wear it out—and, then you will volunteer to buy another one, which will make the authors and their publisher, ABC-CLIO, smile at the book's popularity.

I

The Basics

"Ev'rybody's doin' it. Doin' it, doin' it. Ev'rybody's doin' it. Doin' it, doin' it."
This repetitious phrase is the refrain of Irving Berlin's hastily written 1911 tune designed to exploit America's burgeoning popular dance craze. Berlin's double entendre–titled melody succeeded hugely: "Everybody's Doin' It" became the generic anthem for the dance mania of the early twentieth century.[1]

We have borrowed Berlin's phrasing of this song to characterize what has been happening to volunteer participation in our own times. Volunteerism has exploded in recent decades. Here is some evidence:

- "In 2008, 61.8 million Americans or 26.4 percent of the adult population contributed 8 billion hours of volunteer service worth $162 billion, using [a] . . . 2008 estimate of the dollar value of a volunteer hour ($20.25)."[2]
- In 2010: "Volunteers provide[d] a powerful economic and social benefit to communities across the nation, with 62.8 million adults serving almost 8.1 billion hours through organizations. . . . [In the process,] America's volunteers provided services valued at nearly $173 billion to communities."[3]
- In 2010–2011, volunteering increased by 0.5 of 1 percent, lifting the number of volunteers to nearly 65 million. The tabulation dropped by 0.3 of 1 percent in 2011–2012, to 64.5 million volunteers.[4]
- The Bureau of Labor Statistics in September 2011 reported that more than one out of every four Americans volunteered in the previous year.[5]

And all the volunteer numbers, with a few exceptions, just keep climbing. Everyone is "doing it." Everyone is using volunteers.

Susan J. Ellis and Katherine H. Campbell, authors and consultants in volunteer-ism, conclude that "volunteering is so pervasive in the United States that it can be observed daily in almost every aspect of life, from giving blood to handing out political leaflets. The problem is that volunteering, because it is so pervasive, often goes unrecognized."[6]

Adding to the subject's haziness is the reality that volunteer lifestyles have changed. Gone are all those stay-at-home moms who now not only work for a living and operate one-parent households, but also head organizations—including libra-ries of all sizes. Another factor in obscuring the volunteer landscape is what has happened to the huge numbers of Elks, Moose, Rotarians, Lions, and others like them from the once-mighty national service organizations whose strength has ebbed away because of changing lifestyles, aging, retirement, and death. And, along with the dramatic demographic shifts labeled with terms such as "boomers" and "gen-Xers" are the equally jarring technology shifts, as small handheld devices replace writing and print as the principal tools of interpersonal communication and persuasion. Technology, too, has affected the shape of American volunteerism, bringing the term "virtual volunteer" into existence by the mid-1990s.

A father-son team writing on how to use volunteers in faith-based organizations highlights the differences in volunteerism from previous decades. They note, "More than ever, today's volunteers work online, need flexible hours, and want to play a role in defining their jobs. They also want to feel a sense of responsibility for your organization's overall mission." After this description comes the religious leaders' exhortation: "Harness this passion and potential—with results that uplift your goals and enable your volunteers."[7] That's good advice for all not-for-profits—including libraries.

WHAT IS A VOLUNTEER?

In writing this book, we became convinced once more that the term "volunteer" is related in its nuances to Winston Churchill's 1939 comment about what Russia would do if attacked by Germany. Churchill demurred to predict the future, remarking that "I cannot forecast to you the action of Russia. It is a riddle wrapped in a mystery inside an enigma."[8] That relationship is because there is more agree-ment about what a volunteer is than about what a volunteer does, especially what such a person does in a library. Here are the word's origins and some definitions.

"Volunteer" comes via the French *volontaire* from the Latin *voluntārius*, a noun use of the adjective that gave English the word "voluntary" (fourteenth century). This was derived from the noun *voluntās*, "will, free will," which itself was based on *volō*, "I will" (also the source of English "volition"). To sum up, the origin and essence of volunteerism is in the free will of the person volunteering.[9] This is a good point to remember. To reiterate, to volunteer is an act of free will.

From one textbook on the subject comes this definition: "Volunteering is rela-tively uncoerced. . . . is intended to help. . . . [and] is done without primary or imme-diate thought of financial gain. . . . The activity is work, not play."[10] There is a bit of a problem here, because many libraries benefit from "coerced volunteerism" (These are court-mandated or institutionally mandated volunteer terms. You'll find more on that in later chapters of this book.) From the volunteer community comes this definition: "Volunteers are persons age 16 and older who serve through or with an organization without pay at any point during a 12 month-period."[11]

Some libraries add to this definition by allowing persons under 16 to undertake volunteer tasks. If you are involved in using youth volunteers, take a look at a later subsection of this volume called "Using Child Volunteers." Some public safety and common-sense operating rules are not optional for volunteers working for your institution. That is especially true for kids, whom the law defines as being at risk in several different ways, especially when adults are getting paid to work around their volunteer efforts.

Finally, there is the legal definition, which always is a good place to start almost any library work task. In legal terms, a volunteer is "a person who does some act or enters into a transaction without being under any legal obligation to do so and without being promised any remuneration for his/her services."[12]

Now, with this multiplicity of nuance—or confusion—why should libraries want to induce volunteers into the midst of their organizations. For a good answer, we return to Churchill's quote, this time adding an important nuance that actually is part of the quote. Churchill's remark reads: "I cannot forecast to you the action of Russia. It is a riddle wrapped in a mystery inside an enigma, but perhaps there is a key. That key is **Russian national interest**" (emphasis added). In the case of libraries, the key ought to be "institutional self-interest." Volunteers can help librarians a lot. But the library professionals need to know what they're doing when they start using volunteers or when they try to add more. Chapter 4 helps define your library's volunteer needs.

THE AMERICAN VOLUNTEER LEGACY

As they set out to create new or reformed volunteer programs, American libraries have a great legacy on which to build. Seeking out and organizing volunteers is as old as the United States, and as American as apple pie. There are lots of ways to start the story of American library volunteerism; our way of starting is through the observation of a keen-eyed Frenchman.

About the time that many public and academic libraries were formalizing their operations in the 1830s, French writer and political philosopher Alexis de Tocqueville produced an insightful portrait of the new United States of America. Issued in Europe in two volumes in 1835 and 1838, de Tocqueville declared volunteerism to be one of the most noteworthy features of American community behavior. According to de Tocqueville, the population of this "most democratic country on the face of the earth" treated volunteerism as a "new science to the greatest number of purposes." In the process, de Tocqueville documented volunteerism as a prolific and characteristic form of community problem-solving.

The French observer noted, "The Americans make associations to give entertainments, to found seminaries, to build inns, to construct churches, **to diffuse books**, to send missionaries to the antipodes[13]; in this manner they found hospitals, prisons, and schools" (emphasis added).[14] "To diffuse books" was as close as de Tocqueville came to using the word "library." But as a highly educated European, he recognized the diffusion of printed books as a critical mechanism to broaden the nation's knowledge.

Americans choose to organize such volunteer activities out of necessity. Without aristocracy, gentry, or even a fully established merchant elite, individuals who sensed a need gathered volunteers to become more powerful—to speak with a united voice or to take action when no single person alone could handle a particular task.[15] In short, volunteerism, according to de Tocqueville, was a much-used form of community building. In more recent times, he might have regarded it as a visible feature of the much-examined American character as some later historians have done.[16]

VOLUNTEER LIBRARY USERS

American libraries began in the voluntary tradition; in modern times, they continue to develop within a strong voluntary heritage. A couple of years ago, a person writing on the Internet about the Sullivan (New York) Free Library did an electronic post on what staff ought to call the individuals and families who used the library. The blogger suggested that the choice was among the terms of "patron," "customer," "user," or "member."[17] There is a larger rubric that covers all users in most libraries. That categorical word is "volunteer." And, that term is almost always correct because it is the rare exception when most people in any single group are forced to use a particular library—or, for that matter, any library.

The possible exceptions come perhaps when a professor assigns research to an assistant, a teacher pushes kids to learn how to use particular electronic databases, a business executive demands "just right" quotes for a speech, a harried doctor pushes a younger doctor to check a symptomology or an etiology, or some other example of assignment or coerced task. These required assignments aside, most users choose when and how to use the library. To quote from the Sullivan mission statement, the library provides "materials and services for their recreational, educational, informational, cultural and civic needs. . . . **The library provides the alternatives, the user makes the choices**" (emphasis added).[18]

This statement gets the position of the cart and the horse exactly right: Users who selectively "choose" what institution, organization, or business to use for any service or product are volunteers in the same sense that shoppers become buyers in stores or service agencies. All sorts of persons can choose to use a particular library in droves or walk or drive right by and never come in. The options presented by computer technology and the Internet only add more choices to a user's process of choice.

No other service organizations are more volunteer-dependent than libraries. Examples abound. In the late 1980s, for example, the St. Louis Public Library (SLPL) had fewer than 350 children participating in summer reading. SLPL board members and administrators decided that the library shouldn't hide behind community statistics: The city of St. Louis was nearly 50 percent black and had over 50 percent of its households living in poverty, with nearly 50 percent of adults officially recognized as having "literacy problems" that held them back in the workplace. Working through those issues, SLPL staff conceptualized the city's youth as a needy "latent market" and set out to get local youth to "choose" to come to the library and engage in summer reading.

Working through those issues, by the summer of 2002, SLPL involved 24,000 children from babes in arms to 18-year-olds in summer reading. This shift in numbers from a few hundred to many thousands—from fewer than 1 out of 100 children to 1 out of 3.5 children—did not happen by magic but because of specific administrative direction that certain library staff "work the streets."

The tactic that won the most new kid volunteer users was "to go to them where they are," an outreach effort that *American Libraries* columnist Joseph Janes reminds librarians is a critical element in why users set out to use the institution's products and services. Going to them means going to their homes, offices, daycare centers, clubs, schools, churches, and web cafes personally, in print and virtually, to carry the message that the library is a place for them to study, recreate, and, yes, even meet socially. The essential outreach message is that your library has what kid users want, and that the public library was *the place* where youth—from little kids to teen gang entrepreneurs—should spend some summer time to pursue their reading and information interests via books, magazines, and lots of computers.[19]

The St. Louis Cardinals baseball club provided dramatic support to this effort to get youth to choose the library for summertime recreation. The Cardinals provided the library with 6,000 tickets (3,000 pairs) so that an adult and a child summer reader could attend a free Cardinals baseball game, plus bats, gloves, T-shirts, and radio advertising timeslots on the Cardinals Network. And because of connections through the Cardinals' electronic stations, the kids also received free McDonald's meals and free time playing game machines at electronic arcades. In other words, without guilt, our staff used material incentives to help kids decide that they might find something at the library that was worth their time. The library helped them become voluntary users.

As library summer reading burgeoned, so too did attendance in year-round youth and adult activities. It became a library truism to note that if adults would follow their kids to McDonald's to buy them Happy Meals, they would follow them to the library and to the Cardinals' stadium to be honored as participants in the library's Summer Reading Program. The other part of the outreach message was that summer reading was family-centered and would help kids become successful in school and adult-life ready.

Gay Ivey, a professor of reading education at James Madison University in Virginia, says that libraries shouldn't act like school classes and push all children and adults to read the same book. The real world, Ivey says, is far more varied. All reading research shows that very successful, educated, productive people don't read the same things in their adult lives. When you look at how they use libraries and book stores, such persons "aren't breaking down the doors of Barnes & Noble to get a copy of *The Scarlet Letter*."[20]

To make such statements about volunteer children users and volunteer adult users who are not wealthy or well educated is to admit openly that libraries are *not* required. And, like it or not, whether the institution is a university research facility, a special library, or a public, school, or corporate library, the essential point is that even if potential users have "a library assignment," they may decide to use or not to use a particular library to complete that assignment. That was true before the Internet, and it is truer now. In short, library users have the freedom to choose. They can choose the library or not. In short, they volunteer.

Former Baltimore County Library system director Charlie Robinson recognized the reality of customer-driven libraries before many others did. "I have always looked at libraries from the point of view of the [patron] rather than the librarian," he says. One of Robinson's favorite rules for library success is: "Give the people what they want, not what librarians feel they should want." That, in his mind, was the only way to keep the voluntary users coming back to use his Baltimore County branches.[21]

To sum up, the diffusion of books to which de Tocqueville referred in the 1830s remains a central but expanded activity today. Whether the outreach or extension is to preschools, adults working in the outback, homework help for school-age kids and college students or outreach to researchers, seniors or prisoners, the message is the same: There is value, as in fun and/or personal growth, in using the library. But users must volunteer to make use of those resources. To quote the Sullivan mission statement one more time, "The library provides the alternatives, the user makes the choices."

The best way to understand libraries—both their failures and their successes—is to recognize just how dependent they are on volunteer users. If library attendance was like that of school attendance, libraries (including school libraries) would be less dependent on volunteer users. If libraries were like police, fire departments, or sewers, water and electricity users, they would have a different evolutionary history because all of these services have times when citizens must use them. There are no options.

Corporate libraries, denominational libraries, rare books libraries, government agency libraries, specialized medical libraries, art and history museum libraries— all these share with academic and public libraries a dependence on users who choose to use them, and all worry rightfully over those who do not. This voluntaristic nature sets libraries apart from other civic and educational institutions.

Because of their very nature, then, libraries have a special place in America's voluntary tradition. Not only are their users volunteers, but many (even most) libraries were advocated for, founded, funded, and operated by volunteers. In addition, the operation of a purposeful, results-oriented volunteer program brings a range of citizens into library service that can lead to increased support. In short, volunteers who have a positive experience working for a library become informal and even formal advocates for the library's organizational and funding needs. Both of these subjects are explored in more detail in the next two chapters.

INFRASTRUCTURE IS CRITICAL

You undoubtedly have heard the old cliché, "You are what you eat," a crude saying devised from the scientific claims of a French physician trying to stop gout in the early nineteenth century.[22] In the case of both paid staff and volunteers alike, there is this truth: "Your library is defined by who does what, when and how!" Which is another way of saying, "A good volunteer can make your library look like a great institution; a bad volunteer can bring public retribution to your organization faster than firing a popular director."

For libraries—just as for other kinds of organizations throughout the United States—there is one huge problem other than shifting lifestyle changes based on seismic shudders in demographics and technology. A document prepared by the Volunteer Generation Fund in 2009 provided the critical clue: "There are millions of people ready to serve. . . . but the challenge before us . . . is this: Do we have the infrastructure, in our nonprofit sector, to meet the demand? Are we constructing a secure foundation to connect those willing to serve to meaningful, results-driven volunteer activities?"[23] These questions are the most important ones that library leaders need to ask when setting up or reforming a volunteer program. The worlds of work and of leisure are changing faster than institutions—including libraries—can keep up with them. Volunteerism is a good way to help adjust institutions for the future.

Much of the remainder of this book focuses on creating the critical infrastructure to make volunteerism successful within libraries and to make volunteers so happy about their library volunteer experience that they spread your positive message to friends and family members alike. When your library operates that kind of a volunteer program, you will have experienced the main reasons that volunteers are so important to all kinds of libraries.

NOTES

1. Songfacts, from http://www.songfacts.com/detail.php?id=13547 (accessed October 22, 2012).

2. Corporation for National and Community Service (CNCS), http://www.nationalservice .gov/about/role_impact/performance_research.asp#VIA_2011 (accessed November 9, 2012).

3. Ibid.

4. U.S. Bureau of Labor Statistics, *Volunteering in the United States, 2012* (Washington, DC: BLS, February 22, 2012), http://www.bls.gov/news.release/volun.nr0.htm (accessed July 11, 2013).

5. U.S. Bureau of Labor Statistics, *Volunteering in the United States, 2011* (Washington, DC: BLS, February 22, 2013), http://www.bls.gov/news.release/volun.nr0.htm http://www.bls.gov/ news.release/archives/volun_02222012.pdf (accessed July 11, 2013).

6. Susan J. Ellis and Katherine H. Campbell, *By the People: A History of Americans as Volunteers*, New Century (3rd) ed. (Philadelphia: Energize, Inc., 2006). Quote from Amazon intro, probably authors' preface or intro.

7. Jonathan McKee and Thomas W. McKee, *The New Breed: Understanding & Equipping the 21st Century Volunteer* (Loveland, CO: Ministry Essentials, 2007).

8. "A Riddle Wrapped in a Mystery Inside an Enigma," *TVTropes*, http://tvtropes.org/ pmwiki/pmwiki.php/Main/ARiddleWrappedInAMysteryInsideAnEnigma (accessed March 6, 2013).

9. Word Origins.com, http://www.merriam-webster.com/dictionary/volunteer (accessed April 3, 2011).

10. From Dr. Ivan Scheier. Cited in Steve McCurley and Rick Lynch, *Volunteer Management: Mobilizing All the Resources of the Community* (Darien, IL: Heritage Arts, 1996), 1.

11. CNCS, "Volunteering," 2009.

12. *Online Free Dictionary*, http://www.thefreedictionary.com/volunteer (accessed January 4, 2012).

13. The Antipodes are a group of rocky islands of the southern Pacific Ocean southeast of New Zealand, to which they belong. They were discovered by British seamen in 1800 and are so named because they are diametrically opposite Greenwich, England. De Tocqueville is resorting to contemporary common informal usage. For him, like other literate persons of his time, the Antipodes were Australia and New Zealand.

14. Alexis de Tocqueville, "Of the Use Which the Americans Make of Public Associations in Civil Life," *Democracy in America*, vol. 2, chap. 5, http://xroads.virginia.edu/~HYPER/DETOC/toc_indx.Html (accessed January 17, 2010).

15. Ibid.

16. See, for example, Daniel J. Boorstin, *The Genius of American Politics* (Chicago: University of Chicago Press, 1953), in which the author puts the public library, the general store, and the volunteer fire department in the same sentence as prime examples of the inventive genius of America. The quote is easiest in accessibility in an early excerpt at http://teachingamericanhistory.org/library/index.asp?document=2203.

17. "What Do You Call People Who Use the Library?" *Sullivan* (NY) *Free Library Blog*, posted July 1, 2010, http://sullivanfreelibrary.wordpress.com/2010/07/01/what-do-you-call-people-who-use-the-library/ (accessed January 8, 2013).

18. Sullivan (NY) Free Library home page, http://midyorklib.org/sullivan/ (accessed January 8, 2013).

19. Joseph James, "Internet Librarian: Technology. The Right Question: Knowing what to ask is the first step in facing the future." *American Libraries*, September 2008, 47.

20. Erin Anderson, "Letting Students Choose Books Could Make Them Better Readers," *Globe and Mail*, March 29, 2010, updated August 23, 2012. http://www.theglobeandmail.com/news/national/education/letting-students-choose-books-could-make-them-better-readers/article570697/ (accessed April 24, 2013).

21. "The Mad Librarian," *Baltimore Magazine*, January 1995, http://www.joabj.com/Balt/9501Librarian.html (accessed January 8, 2013).

22. "You are what you eat" is a translation of the French phrase "Dis-moi ce que tu manges, je te dirai ce que tu es" (Tell me what you eat and I will tell you what you are), written by French doctor Anthelme Brillat-Savarin in *Physiologie du Gout, ou Meditations de Gastronomie Transcendante* (1826). http://answers.yahoo.com/question/index?qid=20091019011837AAu7XE0 (accessed April 19, 2013).

23. Reimagining Service, "If We Build It, They Will Come: The Imperative for Strengthening the Nation's Volunteer Infrastructure," http://www.reimaginingservice.org/sites/default/files/u17/POL_Vol_Generation_Fund.pdf (accessed January 1, 2013).

2

Hidden Volunteers

When librarians speak or write about a library's "hidden volunteers," they usually treat them as discrete groups under their usual categorical names: library founders, trustees, fund-raisers or advocates separate from the institution's more visible "volunteer program." Because of their importance in library life and because they require many—or even more—"volunteer services" and training than better-known volunteer groups, they deserve special attention early in this book.

Hidden volunteers are usually involved in most of the critical moments of American libraries. And, many—even most—of those critical moments do not take place at a library service desk, in front of a library shelf, or even within a library building. Instead, hidden volunteers work their magic in offices, clubs, restaurants, meeting rooms, and living rooms.

The work of hidden volunteers always involves words—sometimes written, more often spoken. And, they involve promises and commitments that usually are kept—the gift of a treasured book or manuscript collection, the writing of checks that have more than a couple of zeros after other numbers, and plaques, naming opportunities, testimonial dinners, and mentions in obituaries of a prominent or obscure name without whom this or that library would have had a far lesser history.

Hidden volunteers give their personal and corporate wealth to start libraries; they push legislatures or private-sector boards of directors to start or to advance funds for libraries. They press their friends to sit on library boards and advisory committees. And, along with financial resources and their community connections, they give their own time to help professionals achieve visions of community service that they may not even have thought about without advocacy from noninstitutional voices.

The contributions of hidden volunteers only sometimes, if ever, make it into a public spotlight. Good, important work usually attracts less publicity than a service breakdown, a criminal act committed in or near a library, the protests of irate citizens who want to eliminate an "obscene" sex act, racial stereotyping, ethnic profiling from library books or library computers, or branch closings because of lack of funds.

In spite of their significant work for libraries, the assemblages of hidden volunteers who in the past and present create critical connections among libraries and their communities exist in every type of library. Because of their importance, it is worth calling attention to them here.

VOLUNTEERS START LIBRARIES

The first group of hidden volunteers is those who start libraries. Circumstance and a particular ideological mind-set have led Americans to create many institutions. Throughout its history, the United States has been short on the skills and resources it has needed to undertake new tasks, many of them undefined as to the work involved. Volunteering to do the undefined, whether creating a new organization or perfecting a different kind of machine is characteristic of American development, as Jack Hitt points out in his highly readable volume, *Bunch of Amateurs.*[1]

For example, most social services—including help for the poor, care for the sick, and assistance for orphaned children—were handled by volunteers before they were institutionalized and/or professionalized.[2] The roots of library advocacy, for example, began when volunteers were everything because a library was nothing since it did not yet exist.[3]

To begin at the beginning, volunteers start libraries. English clergyman John Harvard's bequest of 400 books was the start of the Harvard University library system. Like many other early libraries, it was a research collection selected by its owner.[4] Sometimes such libraries were set up to expand study possibilities for undergraduate or graduate students, but more often to create research collections. Volunteers, whether faculty or benevolent donors, started libraries on college campuses because no library previously existed there.

Former Microsoft executive John Wood exemplifies the American library founding tradition though his libraries are outside U.S. borders. After exiting Microsoft, Wood set off on a walking trip that turned into a huge project to found libraries for children in third-world countries. Wood wrote a book about his experiences, from a marketing director through his decision to launch the not-for-profit Room to Read, which started over 2,000 schools and libraries for Asian children.[5] His more recent book highlights the expanded work of his school- and library-founding organization.[6]

Linda S. Fox, now director of Capitan Public Library in Capitan, New Mexico, tells a different kind of founding story—how a small group of volunteers determined roles, mission, and planning priorities to create their community's library, which they now operate with Fox as its head. Fox's account is a good place for those wanting to start libraries to examine the steps in their own libraries' creation.[7]

Such volunteer-founding stories continue to be written. One notable recent example is from Stevens County, Washington, where volunteers acted to transfer a hodgepodge of collections into a functioning library system.[8] Another founding occurred in the mid-1970s, when one of the authors of this volume watched as a volunteer spent much of one summer organizing a research library and archives for the National Museum of Transport in St. Louis. Although this library was begun as an in-house research resource, transportation scholars quickly found the small but highly organized collection. The volunteer literally created the library out of piles of books, assembling donations, cataloging materials, and arranging volumes on shelves.

Professional librarians often are involved in these start-ups. One of the authors of this volume helped organize a library of 10,000 books for grades preschool through sixth grade in a St. Louis inner-city private school. Volunteers organized book and other material donations and raised funds for an electronic catalog, and parents helped shelve books. Librarian volunteers also cataloged materials and trained teachers in collection development. This library quickly became the heart of the little inner-city academy, handling literacy, learning, and research and providing instruction in reading and computer-based research as well. A similar process is recounted by a St. Charles, Missouri, librarian explaining how she and other librarians use their professional expertise to start libraries for churches, schools, and other organizations, going through the start-up process from the volunteer's side.[9]

ALA officially recognizes volunteers (both with and without prior professional training or expertise) who found libraries on its Internet web pages. "Setting Up a Special Library" is recognized as a valuable activity, which it aids with the electronic publication of "Setting Up a Special Library: A Resource Guide," Fact Sheet 16C. This document functions as a primer for how individuals can start all kinds of libraries. It acknowledges the variety of library foundings, including those in business offices and special research collections. ALA also considers the probability that some founders will be trying "to set up a library where there is, at the beginning, only the desire to have library service where there is none, such as in a village where a Peace Corps volunteer is working." ALA warns about the complexities involved in organizing a new library and offers what can be regarded as an outline for the course, Library Organization 101, as the way to ease the process.[10] That overview is followed by a short bibliography entitled "General resources for any small library."[11]

ALA also recognizes that some kinds of special libraries require special requirements, a reality that is aided by organizational advice from the Special Libraries Association, the Medical Library Association, and many other library groups. These efforts are also aided by institutional publications like the University of South Carolina's "Starting a Special Library from Scratch," which is an outline even more basic than ALA's Fact Sheet 16C.[12] The large numbers of such helpful publications for starting a library is an indication that library start-ups are still a huge voluntary activity.

VOLUNTEERS GOVERN LIBRARIES

To a greater or lesser degree, volunteers who serve on library trustee boards or on various policy advisory committees are often overlooked as important—even the most important—library volunteers. Much of the institutional success depends on the quality of decision making by those who govern. This responsibility is large, especially given the reality that most library governance officials serve without compensation, not even receiving mileage reimbursement for library meeting attendance.

Governing boards that have real authority can undertake many different kinds of activities to aid in the development and sustenance of other library volunteers. They, for example, can ensure that volunteer programs have good oversight, quality leadership, and financial resources rather than being starved for attention, supervision, training, and funding. Far better than many library directors, trustees can keep volunteer programs from overextending or just flat out going off the rails to the detriment of volunteer and library reputations.[13]

The legal responsibilities are especially demanding if the institution is a public library that usually follows legal requirements in state law. Now a bit dated but still very useful, library trustee Virginia Young's multiple editions of her manuals on public library management, a series of ALA editions that began in the mid-1960s, still contain lots of useful organizational ideas.[14]

Many states have excellent trustee manuals as well.[15] The Iowa trustee manual, which is organized as an instructional text for training trustees in their rights and responsibilities, notes that Iowa public library boards have the power to do the following:

- Hire and evaluate the library director and determine compensation for the director and other staff.
- Establish the library's budget within the city council–imposed funding limits.
- Approve and oversee spending.
- Plan for the library's future and adopt policies affecting operations.
- Exercise general oversight and governance of the library's operation.

Alice Korngold, a powerful voice in how corporations should handle their volunteers, says that executives from the business world are often pushed to go on not-for-profit boards to get the training they need to move up in their own companies. Her point is significant because Korngold assumes that not-for-profit trustees will receive training on the job.[16] Many—even most—of those who are appointed or elected to such posts bring with them a strong belief that something the library does needs to be corrected and that they as individual board members can and should do the correcting. The weakness of appointed governing boards is their often thin knowledge about how to operate a successful modern library. The need to overcome that weakness makes trustee education an important staff responsibility, one burdened by the necessity for trustees to have all the facts they need to make appropriate decisions, not just policies favorable to staff.

Another issue is board expectations about how executive staff will lead and manage. Some board members want leadership placidity. Others want high visibility and visionary change. Whatever their desired style of management, governance officials need to recognize that "if worthwhile change is occurring in any institution, director conflicts with the public, staff and the board are as inevitable as arguments between a loving husband and wife or a caring parent and a developing child." There also is a tendency for proactive board members to micromanage institutional life. Board and management relationships are most effective when there is shared power and honest communication.[17]

Though not as clear-cut as in public libraries, other types of libraries have policy-making or at least policy-advisement boards or committees. So too do school libraries. Academic libraries have faculty advisory committees, school media center librarians consult with teachers and parents, and special librarians who operate corporate libraries often consult formally with their management funders and their researcher-users. Governmental libraries have advisory boards as well. Many of these have a basis in law or formal, written policy. If not that, they are based in the reality of good practice.

While treating governing officials with the friendliness, appreciation, and courtesy they deserve for taking on a difficult task, staff must recognize that their most important and ongoing job is to educate board members in such a way that they can make sound decisions about policy and procedures that affect library operations and relationships with constituents. The staff has an obligation to help boards and advisory committees make good decisions so that their library can become or remain successful as it moves forward. That means (1) helping board members, especially new members, recognize the "style" in which their library operates; (2) helping board members understand their powers; (3) helping them figure out that what they think they know is different from what they know and don't know; and (4) helping them recognize the limits of their decision making.

There is a huge literature on the workings of library advisory boards covering faculty, members, and citizens. A simple Google search on this topic brings up millions of hits. In varying degrees, they will tell you the same thing as we noted as generalizations about library boards. One convenient, helpful beginning bibliography on boards is on the Energize website.[18]

Finally, staff needs to ensure that board members understand their legal rights and protections. Directors' and officers' insurance is one form of protection that many library boards sometimes forget; the negotiations with an insurer to bring that protection to library board members helps remind them of the protections they have because they are *not* paid. The American Bar Association has an excellent summary of D&O insurance for nonprofit boards.[19] The other board function that is tightly regulated by law is governance behavior during an audit. The 2002 Sarbanes-Oxley law has rigid legal guidelines that board members must follow when they handle the library's annual audit.[20]

VOLUNTEERS FIND FUNDING FOR LIBRARIES

Too often, many (even most) library staff and their governance officials are sure they have no responsibility for fund-raising. They see "running the library" as separate from finding the money to run a successful library. Nothing, of course, could be further from today's economic realities.

ALA's basic publication on this subject notes: "Library fundraising takes place every day and at all levels of complexity, from the smallest library's book or bake sale to the large urban library's multimillion dollar capital campaign."[21] Everyone associated with a library that needs money is a fund-raiser. And, since most libraries need more funding, almost all of them engage in some form of income generation and money raising. Within such efforts, volunteers nearly always play a significant role. If you are new to fund raising, a recent ALA bibliography on fund-raising basics and titled "Library Fact Sheet No. 24" is a good place to begin conceptualizing staff and volunteer roles.[22]

There are no secrets to successful fund-raising—just a reasonably well-developed pathway of rules and lots of hard work by staff and volunteers as they walk those paths. The process begins with the development of a fund-raising culture within the whole organization.[23] Volunteers are an important part of that effort, especially if the library has not done major fund-raising previously. Volunteers can help you understand the community's fund-raising style and give you leads on prospective donors who should be cultivated. They often bring experience in developing a case statement that is a rationale of need and the community benefits that will ensue from the funds. As the fund-raising culture matures, you usually can find volunteers who will participate in donor cultivation and solicitation.

The authors' St. Louis library experience with fund-raising started with Friends fund-raising with special events. Then staff learned how to write proposals for major research grants like those delivered by LSTA and the much smaller annual incentive grants for special projects that came through the Missouri State Library. In the meantime, the library passed two tax referenda increases in less than four years, tripling operating revenue over the next decade, which allowed the rehabbing or construction of many new branch buildings. Eventually SLPL fund-raising resorted to the sale of bonds to rehab the 100-year-old Central Library. Volunteers—a specialist in tax law, political leaders, foundation board members, high-level corporate leaders, and members of the library's board—all helped find millions of dollars in new revenue.

Fund-raising in small and rural libraries starts with exactly the same kinds of issues that St. Louis faced. ALA has published a useful summary guide to help such libraries in "The Small but Powerful Guide to Winning Big Support for Your Rural Library."[24] Unfortunately, there is scant attention to volunteers in this little guide. In his presentations to small libraries, John Howard of the Illinois Alliance Partnership notes how fund-raising needs to involve many different groups, including "Board Members, Volunteers, Patrons, Donors, Community-minded citizens and People who say yes."[25] He says, "Voluntary involvement in your mission moves volunteers from interest to involvement to ownership."[26]

Volunteers play a large role in all successful fund-raising projects. The Library Friends at the University of Illinois at Champaign-Urbana receive bulk mail, electronic mail, and web page solicitations asking for regular support of the U of I Foundation/Library Annual Fund.[27] Newberry Library in Chicago uses volunteers in a different way: They hold an annual book sale conducted under terms specified in a published guide, which demonstrates considerable thought and excellent writing. It is a useful manual for any library using volunteers at a well-populated book sale.[28] This event should be recognized in the context of the whole Newberry Volunteers Program, which began in 1974 and which has "provided valuable help in development, educational and outreach mailing processes in a time of shrinking library resources."[29]

A different style, also involving volunteers, is carried on by Jean Krause, the director of the Madison County Public Library in Marshall, North Carolina. She says that "Visibility and partnerships are key to successful fundraising." She speaks often at civic club meetings, and she and some of her staff participate in the car washes, bake sales and other fund-raising activities of other organizations. Those appearances increase visibility and make it easier to recruit its fund-raising volunteers. In addition, Krause regularly speaks at civic club meetings and has joined community organizations and supported their fund-raising activities. By participating in other groups' car washes, bake sales, and other activities, Krause finds it easier to get help when the library conducts its own fund-raisers.

Madison County demonstrated another strategy when they were attempting to create a fund-raising committee. "Library staff developed a 'wish list' of individuals who they wanted on the committee. They then contacted each individually with letters and follow-up phone calls." The invitation to attend the first meeting attracted one-third of those asked. In addition, one local banker on the committee organized a golf tournament to benefit the library and obtained a donation from his bank. Such successes demonstrate that even smaller libraries can be highly successful fund-raisers.[30]

To review, libraries need to build a fund raising culture that matches the fund-raising style of the communities where the money is to be solicited. To be successful, that fund-raising needs to involve volunteers—as both solicitors and donors. An important part of fund-raising is finding the positive way to tell the library's story, as in "Here is what the library will do with money for new books or funds for rehabbing branches." Few people like to give money to institutions where the death rattle already is sounding.

Author Ilona Bray, in a for-profit book, provides some excellent advice for successful fund-raising including that of libraries. A few of her major volunteer fund raising points follow.

- Not everyone knows how short the organization is on money for new books or a new carpet unless you tell them. Good communication is the first prerequisite of good fund raising.
- Make sure that your communications are appreciated, not resented, especially e-mail communications. Let persons opt out of e-mail solicitations at any time. Also, keep fund-raising messages short.
- In all communications, especially those in social media like Facebook, create opportunities for interaction by asking questions and getting responses.
- Ask Facebook volunteers to take photos to put on the library's Facebook page, like Louisville Public Library did.
- Line up corporate matching grants, which not only provides more money but also heightens the value of the volunteer donation.

There is much more to be learned in Bray's 350-page book and matching CD that includes bonus information.[31] To sum up, Bray suggests that it is imperative that volunteers are involved in your institutional fund-raising efforts.

VOLUNTEERS ADVOCATE FOR LIBRARIES

A strong volunteer program can improve the community reputation of any library. It is well known in the United States that one-on-one and small-group conversations are the most influential way to grow or to change public opinions, including building positive opinions for community fund raising.[32] Such groupings are far more significant than reading a book or a magazine, hearing an advertisement on TV, or seeing it on Facebook.

Volunteering is a great way to learn about library advocacy. In 2010, Cecilia Hogan, the director of University Relations Research at the University of Puget Sound in metropolitan Seattle, wrote, "For the nonprofit, facilitating successful volunteer experiences . . . is a way to build a group of dedicated supporters, some of whom will support the nonprofit with financial gifts one day. We might say that what begins as a transactional relationship becomes transformational for all involved."[33]

Advocacy begins when volunteers talk to others—to those who volunteer in other organizations or who as yet do not volunteer. A good best-practice rule in volunteer management is to pay attention to the community communication significance of your very own enthusiastic volunteers. One way you'll know your volunteers are telling your library's success story is when you have more offers to volunteer than places to install volunteers in your organization.

Given the significance of the connection between volunteering and advocacy, it is surprising to find so much of ALA's *Library Advocate's Handbook* concerns how staff rather than library volunteers should behave in advocacy settings.[34] This publication contains less than half a dozen references recommending the training of users, civic figures, or friends as advocates and suggesting how staff should play a significant part in that training.

This fuzziness can be seen in the recent history of Friends of Libraries USA (FOLUSA). On February 1, 2009, FOLUSA was replaced by the Association of Library Trustees, Advocates, Friends and Foundation (ALTAFF). This unit was made a division of the American Library Association in an attempt to create a more unified push for advocacy within the national library organization.[35] ALTAFF has now evolved into United for Libraries, the Association of Library Trustees, Advocates, Friends and Foundations, which combines governance, advocacy, and friends and foundation fund-raising. Of course, these groups are often disparate in character and sometimes need to be disconnected to keep peace among them.

Any library professional who has testified before a local, state, or national legislative committee knows that paid library staffs are usually treated with no more than cool respect. Legislators often perceive and treat paid staff as self-interested bureaucrats pleading for their own salaries and working conditions, not as influential citizens backing continued or additional funding for libraries. The importance of this point is magnified when public funding pays the salaries of the testifying library staff.[36]

Library advocacy is served best when high-visibility citizens pass on the information, especially if donors are the message bearers and the legislators are sometimes the recipients of their largesse. Even without this obvious economic connection, however, volunteer advocates usually receive more attention than staff.

As there was in the case of library funding, professional staff has a distinct role to play with library board members and advocate volunteers. This role is exemplified in the work of ALA's Office for Library Advocacy (OLA), which "supports the efforts of advocates seeking to improve libraries of all types by developing resources, a peer-to-peer advocacy network, and training for advocates at the local, state and national level."[37] The role of staff in such advocacy is to furnish the research that advocates can use to make critical points. The case for such research has been made by practitioners and scholars for both the United States[38] and Canada.[39]

Every type of library needs its volunteer advocates. One group of library professionals hit by the Great Recession are school librarians/educational media center specialists. Indiana[40] and Oklahoma[41] were two of many states that registered such shortages in local newspapers. So extreme is this shortage that ALA has had difficulty in finding sufficient professional volunteers to fill out its school library/media center committees.[42]

To conclude, at the very least, staff needs to help their institutions find appropriate advocates—all the time, of course, but especially in times when the financial future of the institution is on the line. Moreover, once those persons are chosen and in place, staff, especially management staff, has a responsibility to help train the volunteers so they can be successful at their governance and advocacy activities. Training for board members and library advocates—and communicating regularly with them—is an important part of running a successful library. Hidden volunteers not only need recognition for their significant work, but they need conceptual assistance, help in learning about the institution's service organization, and clerical support to do a good job for the libraries where they conduct their voluntary activities.

VOLUNTEERS HELP PROVIDE CULTURAL DIVERSITY

To these obvious "hidden volunteer" roles, another one needs to be added. That is how volunteers can contribute to cultural diversity. In a nation in which cultural diversity in population increasingly is the norm rather than the exception, libraries often lag in the shift. A Hispanic *Volunteer Match* blogger, Chris Bautista, lays out some of the major issues when he proclaims that, as "a person of color and someone who identifies on the LGBT spectrum," he often felt uncomfortable "with white, middle and upper class people doing what they felt was best for me." He writes, "For those who are being helped, encountering a volunteer of a similar identity is comforting, and may inspire [them] to begin their own community building projects."[43]

Writing on *Volunteer Involvement in California Libraries: Best Practices,* for the California State Library in 1999, Carla Campbell Lehn affirmed the significance of diversity in library volunteer ranks. She argued, "To be as relevant as possible to their communities, many libraries have committed to achieve diversity which reflects the population of their community on their staffs, . . . Boards and in their programming. Volunteers can help make those connections—ask them to help you build relationships across ethnic and age boundaries. The library is a wonderful place to mix generations and cultures."[44]

The director of the Paso Robles (California) Public Library emphasizes how volunteers can shift a library's collective view by the weight of its life experiences. She notes, "Our volunteers bring a much wider range of backgrounds" than staff. "People have work and life experiences that include marketing, computing, medical fields, fine arts, small business, large corporations, banking, grant writing, child care, manufacturing, agriculture and more. This wealth of expertise and talent adds much to our collective knowledge."[45]

A brief quote from the Nevada County (California) Library's *Vision Statement* notes that the organization must "reach out to [the] entire diverse community—must consider geographic issues; different needs of children and youth (i.e., age appropriate materials), elderly (i.e., large print books); computer-literate and non-[literate]."[46]

The San Diego Public Library emphasizes the need for internal harmony in operations. "Volunteers and staff work closely together to accomplish day-to-day tasks. They are expected to respect and value the diversity of co-workers and work cooperatively and effectively with others in team efforts to accomplish the library's goals and objectives with minimal conflicts."[47] Lehn connects with this broadened view of diversity. In addition to addressing ethnic and cultural diversity, she includes sections on involving youth, seniors, families, and people with disabilities as volunteers.[48] Preston Diggers and Eileen Dumas, in the second edition of their book *Managing Library Volunteers*, also favor this expansive view. In their book's index, the "diversity" item says, "See cultural diversity."

Bautista lays out a set of rules for achieving volunteer diversity. Here is a summary version of his list, titled "How to Add a Little More Color to Your Volunteer Set"[49]

- Hire staff who "belong to or identify with" the diverse community served.
- Recruit using media and organizations that serve diverse minorities.
- Photographs in recruiting materials should reflect the community's diversity.
- Recruit "in languages other than English."
- Schedule volunteer participation and events being "mindful of religious observances."
- Allow people served to tell the library what they need, not vice versa.
- Explicitly state in recruitment that you want certain groups to reply, as in "People of color and LGBT individuals are strongly encouraged to volunteer."
- In recruitment and on the library website, always include a highly visible nondiscrimination statement and make it as visible as possible, both digitally and in print.
- Partner with nonprofits who target and serve minorities.
- "If a volunteer opportunity requires bilingual skills," advertise that fact.

Bautista's reference to recruitment in a language other than English caused one informed blog reader, the knowledgeable Susan Ellis, to warn about staff inability to speak a non-English language.[50] Her additional warning: "Do not imply in materials that the organization can speak with someone in their non-English language, if no one actually can."

To complete this point, many libraries still have a lot left to do in establishing a culturally diverse volunteer program. As this section indicates, many unresolved issues great and small float through the issue of cultural diversity among volunteers—and in the library community generally. With diverse groups becoming the service mainstream, the library community needs to pay much more attention to using volunteers to help close what in many organizations has become a huge cultural gap. In the meantime, culturally diverse volunteers remain one more group of the library's "hidden volunteers."

NOTES

1. Jack Hitt, *Bunch of Amateurs: A Search for the American Character* (New York: Crown, 2012).

2. The work and publications of the Foundation Center are an overt proclamation of this significant relationship. See, for example, Foundation Center, *Nonprofit Resources by State*. http://foundationcenter.org/gainknowledge/map/california.html (accessed June 27, 2013).

3. Sharon Gray Weiner, "The History of Academic Libraries in the United States: A Review of the Literature," *Library Philosophy and Practice* 7, no. 2 (Spring 2005), http://www .webpages.uidaho.edu/~mbolin/weiner.htm (accessed July 3, 2011); Orvin Lee Shiflett, "Academic Libraries," in *Encyclopedia of Library History*, ed. Wayne A. Wiegand and Donald G. Davis (New York: Garland, 1994).

4. Wikipedia, "Harvard University Library," http://en.wikipedia.org/wiki/Harvard_University _Library (accessed October 29, 2012).

5. John Wood, *Leaving Microsoft to Change the World: An Entrepreneur's Odyssey to Educate the World's Children* (New York: Harper Business, 2006).

6. John Wood, *Creating Room to Read: A Story of Hope in the Battle for Global Literacy* (New York: Viking Penguin, 2013).

7. Linda S. Fox, *The Volunteer Library: A Handbook* (Jefferson, NC: McFarland, 1999), See also Beth Wheeler Fox, *The Dynamic Community Library* (Chicago: ALA, 1988), and Anne Gervasi and Betty Kay Seibt, *Handbook for Small, Rural, and Emerging Public Libraries* (Phoenix, AZ: Oryx Press, 1988).

8. Brian Mathews, "Transforming a Hodgepodge," *American Libraries* 41, no 10 (October 2010): 4; http://www.americanlibrariesmagazine.org/article/transforming-hodgepodge (accessed August 31, 2013).

9. Michelle L. Budt-Caulk, "Volunteer Librarians: Your Time Is Worth as Much as Money," *American Libraries* 37, no. 1 (January 2006): 38–39, 42.

10. The advice reads, "Establishing a new library, or developing an existing collection of books and other materials into a library, involves several functions: creating the oversight or governance structure, defining the mission and purpose of the organization, securing funding, planning, developing a collection, securing or building an appropriate space, equipping the space, and marketing services. In all cases, planning for the collection should come first." "Setting Up a Special Library: A Resource Guide," ALA Fact Sheet No. 16C, http://www.ala.org/tools/ libfactsheets/alalibraryfactsheet16c (accessed May 13, 2013).

11. Ibid.

12. University of South Carolina, "Starting a Special Library from Scratch," http:// faculty.libsci.sc.edu/bob/class/clis724/SpecialLibrariesHandbook/ScratchIndex_files/ ScratchLibraryIndex.htm (accessed June 27, 2013).

13. Melissa D. Abel, "How Can We Help? Nonprofit Boards and the Volunteer Program," Serviceleader.org, December 2003, http://www.serviceleader.org/instructors/studentpaper8

(accessed March 26, 2013). This significant summary article has been cited for its many different observations in various publications.

14. Virginia G. Young, *The Library Trustee: A Practical Guidebook* (Chicago: ALA, 1964–1995). Chapters and content change from edition to edition. Now somewhat dated because of lack of attention to computer communication and in-library use, but it still contains many useful suggestions.

15. For example, Library of Virginia, *Virginia Public Library Trustee Handbook* (2005), http://www.lva.virginia.gov/lib-edu/ldnd/trustee (accessed January 19, 2013). And, Sandy Dixon, ed., *Iowa Library Trustee's Handbook* (Des Moines: Library Development, State Library of Iowa, 2011). Both are excellent publications that will be helpful to library administrators and trustees.

16. Alice Korngold, "Developing Visionary Leaders," *Leader to Leader* 40 (Spring 2006): 45–50. This article is available on the Leader to Leader Institute website at http://www.hessel beininstitute.org/knowledgecenter/journal.aspx?ArticleID=90 (accessed August 31, 2013).

17. Glen E. Holt, "Contract for All Seasons: Freeing Library Directors to Meet Board Expectations," *The Bottom Line* 8, no. 3 (1995): 31–33.

18. "Boards of Directors and Working with Committees: Books on This Topic [and] Articles and Book Excerpts on This Subject," Energize, http://www.energizeinc.com/art/subj/boards.html (accessed April 1, 2013).

19. Stephen M. Foxman, "Directors and Officers Liability Insurance for Non Profits." *Business Law Today* 18, no. 6 (July–August 2009), http://apps.americanbar.org/buslaw/blt/2009-07-08/foxman.shtml (accessed June 28, 2013).

20. "The Sarbanes-Oxley Act and Implications for Nonprofit Organizations," GuideStar, http://www.guidestar.org/rxa/news/articles/2003/sarbanes-oxley-act-and-implications-for-nonprofit -organizations.aspx (accessed April 12, 2013).

21. "Frontline Fundraising Toolkit," ALA, http://www.ala.org/advocacy/advleg/frontline fundraising (accessed June 3, 2009).

22. "Library Fund Raising: A Selected Annotated Bibliography," ALA Library Fact Sheet No. 24, http://www.ala.org/tools/libfactsheets/alalibraryfactsheet24 (accessed January 19, 2013).

23. Glen E. Holt and Thomas Schlafly, "A Fund-raising Primer for Public Library Trustees," in *The Library Trustee: A Practical Guidebook*, ed. Virginia G. Young, 5th ed. (Chicago: American Library Association, 1995), 80–88.

24. "The Small but Powerful Guide to Winning Big Support for Your Rural Library: Tips and Tools You Can Use from the ALA Committee on Rural, Native and Tribal Libraries of All Kinds, the Association for Rural and Small Libraries and the ALA Office for Literacy and Outreach Services," http://www.ala.org/offices/olos/toolkits/rural (accessed August 31, 2013).

25. John Howard, "Starting and Running a Library Annual Fund," presentation, April 30, 2008, http://www.webjunction.org/content/dam/WebJunction/Documents/illinois/Fundraising -101-Creating-an-Annual-Fund-for-Your-Library.pdf (accessed April 28, 2013).

26. John Howard, "Fund Raising 101: The Basics," presentation February 27, 2008, http://www.webjunction.org/events/illinois/fundraising-101-the-basics.html (accessed April 28, 2013).

27. Library Friends website, University Library, University of Illinois, http://www.library .illinois.edu/friends/ (accessed May 18, 2013).

28. "2012 Book Fair Information: The 28th Annual Newberry Library, Book Fair, July 25 to July 29, 2012," http://www.newberry.org/sites/default/files/textpage-attachments/2012 BookFairVolunteerHandbook.pdf (accessed April 1, 2013).

29. Mary Wyly, "Uncommon Human Resources: The Newberry Library Volunteer Program," *Library Trends* 41, no. 2 (Fall 1992): 316–29.

30. *Staying Connected. A Toolkit to Build Support in the Community for Your Technology Programs* (Seattle, WA: Bill & Melinda Gates Foundation, 2002), chap. 9, 85, http://www.webjunction.org/content/dam/WebJunction/Documents/webjunction/SC-Toolkit-Chapter-9-Raise-Funds.pdf (accessed April 28, 2013).

31. Ilona Bray, *The Volunteers' Guide to Fundraising: Raise Money for Your School, Team, Library or Community Group.* (Berkeley, CA: NOLO, 2011), 155–59.

32. See, for example, Andy Robinson, *How to Raise $500 to $5000 from Almost Anyone: A 1-hour Guide for Board Members, Volunteers, and Staff* (Medford, MA: Emerson & Church, 2004).

33. Cecilia Hogan, "For Our Next (Charitable) Trick, We'll Need a Volunteer," http://www.infotoday.com/searcher/jun10/Hogan.shtml (accessed June 14, 2010).

34. ALA, *Library Advocate's Handbook* (Chicago; ALA, n.d.), http://www.ala.org/offices/sites/ala.org.offices/files/content/ola/2008lah.pdf (accessed January 10, 2013).

35. One form of the announcement was retrieved at http://www.folusa.org/membership/index.php (accessed January 10, 2013).

36. Alan Bundy, "The Modern Public Library: The Very Best Investment Your Community Can Make: An Information, Issues and Discussion Paper for Friends of Libraries Groups in Australia," *Public Library Quarterly* 29, no. 4 (October–December 2010): 323–46.

37. "ALA Office for Library Advocacy (OLA)—Home," http://www.ala.org/offices/ola (accessed November 4, 2012).

38. Donald Elliott, Glen E. Holt, Sterling W. Hayden, and Leslie E. Holt, Measuring Your Library's Value: How to Do a Cost Benefit Analysis for Your Public Library (Chicago: ALA, 2007).

39. A Planning and Management Services and Southern Ontario Library Service, *The Library's Contribution to Your Community*, 2nd ed. (Toronto: Southern Ontario Library Service, March 2007).

40. Anne Kibbler, "Media Specialists in Short Supply," *Herald-Times*, February 11, 2003, http://www.slis.indiana.edu/news/story.php?story_id=559 (accessed November 4, 2012).

41. Courtney Bryce, "Schools Suffer Librarian Shortage: One Edmond School, Deer Creek High School, Receive Exemption [to law requiring certification for library media specialists]," *Edmond* (OK) *Sun*, August 29, 2007, http://www.edmondsun.com/schools/x519221152/Schools-suffer-librarian-shortage (accessed November 4, 2012).

42. Diane Chen, "Volunteer or Give Up the Right to Complain," *Practically Paradise* (blog), October 12, 2008, http://blogs.slj.com/practicallyparadise/2008/10/12/volunteer-or-give-up-the-right-to-complain/ (accessed August 31, 2013).

43. Cristopher Bautista, "Diversity and Nonprofits: How to Add a Little More Color to Your Volunteer Set," *Volunteer Match Blog for Social Change Organizations*, February 2, 2012, http://blogs.volunteermatch.org/engagingvolunteers/2012/02/02/diversity-and-nonprofits-how-to-add-a-little-more-color-to-your-volunteer-set/ (accessed January 12, 2013).

44. Carla Campbell Lehn, "Volunteer Involvement in California Libraries: 'Best Practices' " (Sacramento: California State Library, 1999), 15, http://www.library.ca.gov/lds/getinvolved/docs/F-resources/VolunteerInvolvementInCaliforniaLibraries-BestPractices.pdf (accessed April 25, 2013).

45. Ibid., 16.

46. Ibid., 98.

47. Ibid., 173–74.

48. Ibid., 238.

49. Bautista, "Diversity and Nonprofits."

50. Ibid.

3

Popular Types of Library Volunteers

The relationship between volunteers and libraries always has been dynamic, with a resulting character that—like American democracy itself—is more mélange than a neat replicable structure that others can copy without thoughtful adaptation.

This chapter explores several popular types of volunteer programs. Those citations are illustrative, not comprehensive. A hundred or a thousand more examples of successful library volunteerism would add to variety and this book's length, but citing every type of example was hardly the goal. Rather, the authors have tried to present material that will stand as usable examples of good ideas from which your institution can conceptualize changes in its own volunteer practices. That's because those wanting to start or to improve the quality of their volunteer programs usually begin by thinking about a specific program or service need. As they think about that category, they tend to consider related categories. Taking into account the relationships among such issues leads almost inevitably to planning changes, which is covered in Chapter 4.

VOLUNTEERS LEND EXPERIENCE TO COLLECTIONS

There will never be enough librarians with sufficient expertise to catalog, abstract, or devise metadata pathways or otherwise organize extant, current, or newly created knowledge at the rate that it is being produced, recognized, and compiled. That reality opens the way for the creation of metadata pathways to access knowledge by nonlibrarians, like amateur local historians, genealogists, subject bibliographers, and researchers and collectors of all kinds. Like a specialized group of librarians, these persons add to the richness of recorded knowledge by devising and refining metadata descriptions on discrete materials and objects.

Often such metadata experts are nonlibrarian volunteers who abstract, compile, and review knowledge of particular kinds. Volunteerism also rears its head when librarians want to cooperate beyond the limits of their institutional walls. Frequently a band of librarians will volunteer to work beyond their salaried work or degree-field study. Such little groups of professional volunteers end up benefiting an extensive user group by the way they devise the signposts and pathways into the knowledge.

One specific example of such volunteer assistance comes from the Nutrition Evidence Library in the U.S. Department of Agriculture. The NEL "specializes in conducting systematic reviews to inform nutrition policy and programs for what is obviously demanding specialized intellectual and organizational work." The library's professional staff recruit "a highly qualified group of professionals and graduate students to serve as volunteer Nutrition Evidence Library Abstractors to help . . . expand the NEL." In return, NEL offers increased professional knowledge along with training in literature analysis and enhanced professional exposure.[1]

The same kind of activity goes on in local libraries. In the Everett (Washington) Public Library, a "volunteer archivist," through identification, processing, and scanning is making a photographic collection more accessible.[2] This example stands out for its typicality among libraries with many different purposes and in many different sizes.

One obvious specialty that affects libraries is the huge amount of information about the history of authors, books, and publishing being accumulated by amateurs. Witness Wikipedia, with all its headaches and its startling reference entries to millions of subjects that now have far more numerous and more visible access points than they did in even the most comprehensive text-based encyclopedia. And, in the United States, no visitor can enter the exhibits area of any local museum or county historical society without being told about some individual who has been able to correctly identify photographic locations or the painter of artistic renderings almost entirely from personal knowledge.

Librarians volunteer to take part in the creation of metadata descriptions of many different kinds of collections. The importance of this volunteer activity is demonstrated in the 2011 alliance of EBSCO's NoveList with Goodreads, which serves as a specialized type of Wikipedia for popular fiction. The deal brought "Goodreads's wealth of 11 million book reviews and 110 million ratings will now help librarians answer one of the most frequently asked questions—what do I read next?" The partnership integrated NoveList information into library catalogs using a product called NoveList Select. The EBSCO vision to advance NoveList is "a unified, customized index of an institution's information resources, and a means of accessing all that content from a single search box." Metadata from both internal work within the organization and from external sources is the key to this advance. And, lots of librarians and other volunteers as well played an important role in the creation of significant metadata.[3]

Volunteer librarians in Illinois undertook the same kind of activity in the early 2000s, using their own expertise to benefit not only their own libraries, but other libraries as well. In 2004, "70 volunteer librarians" created "Illinois CLICKS," a statewide portal where librarians arrayed a large collection of websites on many different subjects. Using an LSTA grant to cover expenses, the project brought information about special collections that were previously hard to access to one portal. The volunteer project also made the search for government information easier by creating appropriate links to the Illinois State Library.[4]

VOLUNTEERS PROVIDE LITERACY INSTRUCTION

Improved literacy has been one important assignment in library rationale since they began to develop on the North American continent. The specifics of the assignments varied, expanding and contracting as times and society's needs shifted. With schools under attack currently, pressure on libraries to enhance their literacy instructions grows proportionately. This section explores some of the contributions that various kinds of libraries make to U.S. literacy.

Indianapolis–Marion County Public Library organizes a reading program that recruits teen volunteers to read to other teens who have trouble reading English. Instruction by peers creates a conducive atmosphere as the learners improve their ability to read English.[5] London (Ontario) Public Library does the same kind of instruction with and for high school students, when volunteers conduct one-on-one conversation mentors to help non-English-speaking students conduct conversations in English with peers.[6]

The Austin (Texas) Public Library (APL) takes a different literacy tack. In APL's Talk Time, volunteers have conversations with immigrants who have no or little knowledge of English, helping the newcomers obtain sufficient proficiency to shop, live, and work in a Texas university city. The librarians and volunteers who work with this program find this work fulfilling.[7] The Newport Beach (California) Public Library organizes Volunteer Literacy Tutors who help persons to read, write, and speak better practical English, with special help given to using language on the job, in medical treatment situations, and in other interpersonal relationships.[8] Kenton County (Kentucky) Public Library volunteers "read the same children's book in various languages, moving seamlessly from one language to the next until the same page has been read in all the languages." If needed, other volunteers translate a book into their languages so it can be read to show "simultaneous readings can be conducted in many languages."[9]

This basic literacy reading activity also appears in Odle Middle School in Bellevue, Washington. In this program, volunteers help kids learn academic and reading skills. The school caters to many children from poor families. In 2005, an Odle school librarian suggested that parents could help kids learn to read if the librarian didn't have sufficient time. In six years, the teacher built a cadre of 42 trained volunteers, "including parents, high school students, senior citizens, and local business employees. They've helped hundreds of kids improve their reading skills, pay closer attention in class, and become better researchers."[10]

Cassandra Barnett, a past president of the American Association of School Librarians, says that when students are not available to volunteer in school libraries, parents can be trained to take up the slack. Reshelving, straightening shelves, and even light dusting show the children that their parents care about the library and about books and reading. She cites examples from libraries in several states.[11]

VOLUNTEERS PROVIDE TECHNOLOGY INSTRUCTION

Derived from kids going to libraries to enhance their literacy came the Bill and Melinda Gates–inspired effort to assist adults and children alike, especially those in poor neighborhoods, to learn technology literacy. Out of that inspiration came the massive introduction of new electronic communication and memory machines into libraries with both paid library staff and volunteers serving as instructors. As this program has evolved, volunteers often have provided a level of technology instruction that most library staff members either don't believe they have the time to give or don't have the appropriate technical training to do a good job sorting out the technology that needs to be taught.

The Austin (Texas) Public Library and University of Texas LIS students teach computer skills for job seekers, with the LIS students instructing in a series of computer classes for job seekers at the main public library. Classes cover job searching on the Internet, letter writing, resume writing, interviewing skills, and social networking.[12] Many libraries have gone down similar pathways. These include the District of Columbia Public Library, Fairfax County Public Library, Christiana School District outside Philadelphia, Berkeley (California) Public Education Foundation,[13] Kishwaukee (Wisconsin) Community College[14] and a State of Maine Volunteer Program for Schools and Libraries.[15] The Gates Foundation has been involved in many phases of this effort.[16]

VOLUNTEERS PROVIDE LIFE HELP

The board and management of Salina (Kansas) Public Library were inspired by a similar impetus but thought a different need had to be filled. They decided that the Salina Library needed to become a Lifelong Education Center. These 45–70 classes each "semester" are from a broad range of categories, including health and well-being (tai chi, reflexology, and healthy eating, for example), books and literature (book discussion groups, topic discussions, writing classes), dance and music (ballroom dance, folk harp), languages (Spanish, Chinese, Japanese, sign language), food and cooking (vegetarian cooking, Indian cuisine), and much more. "The classes are a popular offering and encourage library users to learn in a new way— through working with individuals in the community with skills to share. . . . This has been a popular program and has brought new vibrancy to the library. We are referred to by those who participate as a 'cultural center' because of the range of activities we now encompass."[17]

Northland (Pennsylvania) Public Library provided life assistance by helping individuals find volunteer assignments in the community. This event was held in March 2008, when 27 persons attended a wine-and-cheese Volunteer Speed Matching Event at Northland Public Library. NPL hosted this "speed match event . . . [as] a fun way to help match local nonprofits in need of volunteers with community members looking for meaningful volunteer opportunities." A timekeeper rang a bill at three-minute intervals. In an hour and a half, 25 persons had found an organization with which to volunteer, and the library had built its reputation as a community connection point.[18]

Moore Memorial Public Library in Texas City, Texas, provided a different form of life help to youth. In the summer of 2009, volunteers from the Friends assisted with youth programs by offering, "Which Fork Is It?" manners classes featuring correct table settings and proper etiquette for dining with family and friends. Friends volunteers also served as judges for the "Monopoly Marathon," and volunteer cooks provided cookies and sandwiches for a tea party for younger children.[19]

San Jose Public Library and San Jose State University Library partnered to provide a different kind of life help. They got volunteer attorneys from the Pro Bono Project of Silicon Valley to give half-hour free consults on landlord/tenant issues, consumer law, government benefits, and family and employment law, along with immigration and wills and trusts.[20]

VOLUNTEERS KEEP THE LIBRARY FUNCTIONING

The Moore Public Library and the San Jose project raise a policy question: The basic problem of this kind of "issue volunteerism" is that the desire and sometimes the real need for it are endless. Every library has to be careful that its volunteer projects are at the center of and not outside its mission. In the United States, there always is someone who with the best of intentions has one more activity that library staff or library volunteerism could do in addition to all the purposeful work it already is doing. It is this challenge to keep doing more and different kinds of "good" that libraries need to ponder seriously before spinning off resources to handle new assignments.[21]

On the upside of such activities, volunteers helping keep libraries functioning can turn into positive publicity. At Naperville (Illinois) Public Library in 2004, volunteer Barbara Hughes, confined to a scooter, received a feature story in the local press for her exemplary reshelving efforts. In the interview, she declared that she liked reshelving books in the children's section best.[22]

A good example of the positive way political and user pressure can shift what a library is doing with volunteers took place at Milner Library at Illinois State University. The charge came from the Student Government Association (SGA), which stated that Milner needed to be open more hours so that students could study there. In the planning, the Association decided to help the library find student volunteers who would help keep the library open during hours when Milner could not afford a full cadre of regular staff. The effort included recruitment, training, and scheduling. In the process, the library demonstrated its flexibility in the face of student needs, and SGA representatives became effective spokespersons for the importance of the library as an on-campus study facility. And, the SGA held down library costs while boosting the institution's image.

Teens at the Ojai Branch Library in Ventura County (California) Library undertook a more focused volunteer effort with an "Adopt a Dewey" project in 2001. Modeled on the Camden County (New Jersey) "Adopt a Shelf" program, the Ojai Library initiated a program in which teen volunteers agreed to work one hour per week, during which time they kept a Dewey Decimal section in good order. In short, they made fun out of a shelving exercise.[23]

Hospital libraries face similar volunteer issues. With their aid, "librarians receive assistance with routine tasks, such as processing of materials and shelving books. When volunteers do such time-consuming tasks, . . . the librarian is freed to concentrate on library programming and other responsibilities that provide greater benefits to the hospital and patients." A strong training program, freedom to select tasks, and recognition for their labor contribute to high retention rates.[24] Hospital libraries in general face many controversies that affect most library volunteer efforts. These include legal status, competition with paid employees, and the determination of volunteers' value.[25]

LIBRARIAN VOLUNTEERS HELP OTHER LIBRARIANS

Librarians not only support volunteering in their own libraries but practice its arts as a way to help other librarians. One example occurred when ALA held its national convention in New Orleans shortly after Hurricane Katrina had flooded many of the city's libraries. As part of their convention attendance, dozens of librarians shelved and otherwise organized and completed library work that would have taken weeks or months without their volunteer contributions.[26]

Like other professionals, health science and health librarianship librarians also volunteer in areas where their training and work already have made them expert. The New York Online Access to Health (NOAH) bilingual health education project is one example. NOAH provides "online access to high quality full-text consumer health information in English and Spanish that is accurate, timely, relevant and unbiased." NOAH's goal is supported by volunteer librarians from the City University of New York, the Metropolitan New York Library Council, the New York Academy of Medicine Library, and the New York Public Library, the Queens Borough Public Library, and the Brooklyn Public Library.[27]

Another shared-reference collective developed in 2004 when some librarians, other library staff, and library school students launched an effort to answer questions, give directions, and provide accurate information during the Republican National Convention in New York City. So successful was the group during the convention that their effort became an established website.[28] Its members still appear on the street during major political events, and the collective organizes meetings at librarians' conventions, offering itself as an alternative information source to regular libraries.[29]

A more publicized example of librarians helping librarians took place on March 17, 1995, when "the Internet Public Library (IPL) debuted. Created as a project by a University of Michigan LIS class, it includes a ready reference collection, a reference desk staffed by reference librarian volunteers from around the world, access to resources of special interest and links to various electronic books." In January 2010, the students launched the website "ipl2: Information You Can Trust," merging resources from the IPL site with those of the Librarians' Internet Index. The site is hosted by Drexel University's College of Information Science and Technology, supported by a consortium of colleges and universities with programs in information science.[32]

VOLUNTEER SPECIAL PROJECTS HELP CHANGE THE LIBRARY'S FUTURE

Recruiting the right kind of volunteers can enrich the life of the library and advance its direction along lines desired by governors and managers. A volunteer program is a great way to conduct an experimental program to find out how to meet a probable need—or to find out if the institution has or can develop a future program to meet a new need without a huge and untenable investment in time, money, or expertise.

Special projects often are an episodic form of Hidden Volunteers discussed in Chapter 2. By and large, library users are infinitely patient with researchers' questions. One notable example occurred with volunteers helped PhD candidate Anne Beecher research her important doctoral dissertation on way finding in public libraries.[33]

St. Louis Public Library has a recent tradition of making few major service changes without consulting its users. SLPL pollsters, for example, called numerous citizens asking for their voluntary participation in helping define the issues of tax referenda in 1988 and 1991. SLPL also used numerous volunteers to help clarify service issues in about 100 focus groups between 1987 and 2004. SLPL treated volunteers well, offering free library mugs to anyone who finished the nearly-20-minute telephone survey plus a standard focus group participation fee—which many participants promptly donated back to the library.[34]

Another public library known to the authors of this book had a mess in its finance office and, as a matter of good management, needed expertise to find out exactly what was involved in that mess. Following up on this need, a library board member approached a friend in a nationally significant accounting firm, and the firm provided one of its consultant accountants to undertake a very quiet and very thorough audit. The for-profit company donated the costs of paying their staff members to conduct and report the audit without cost to the library, and the institution became the beneficiary of a sizeable volunteer-services gift. Yet another example comes from the authors' experience. A small museum needed a new library building, and a retired local architect donated the planning for a clever and inexpensive library facility.

Of course, because of the huge differences in the way that libraries program and operate, some other system's regular volunteer program can be your special project. Here are some examples of special projects that, through time, may become a regular part of your library's work schedule:

- Child care activities for younger children as their brothers and sisters who are their regular caregivers work in the computer lab or do their library-assisted homework.
- Makers spaces where adults and teens with more technology knowledge help younger children learn how to use the new technology.
- The same thing for technology labs where adults and kids learn how to do e-mail, Facebook, or any other of the social media programs that are changing so rapidly.
- The same thing for Internet gaming sessions.
- A volunteer speaker's bureau that covers community appearances to help spread the word about general and specific library services.
- The same thing for volunteers who ride the library vans to help meet neighborhood demand for materials.
- STEM program help. The United States is facing a shortage of qualified graduates in science, technology, engineering, and math (STEM). If they are not doing so already, recruit volunteers who can help tutor STEM students.

This summary, of course, is no comprehensive catalog of all the different types of volunteerism that libraries use to aid in their operations. Big public libraries may have hundreds or even thousands of volunteers working to help them. Small and specialized libraries may have only one or a few persons volunteering their skills or expertise. We, however, have attempted to provide a sense of the range of such activities.

The best advice about volunteers is to consider the help—and the increased visibility—they may bring to the institution. Never neglect the use of volunteers as one of your principal tools to build use and relationships for your library. As you do so, feel free to think of other innovative volunteer examples, but stay true to carrying out your library mission. In the end, volunteers ought to help your institutional focus, not distend the effort to carry out the library's core mission.

NOTES

1. National Library of Agriculture, "National Evidence Library (NEL) Evidence Abstractor Fact Sheet," posted November 9, 2009, last modified March 14, 2012, http://www.cnpp .usda.gov/Publications/NEL-CallforAbstractors.pdf (accessed April 24, 2013).

2. Justin Arnold, "She Deciphers Everett's Past: Library Volunteer Sorts through Historic Photos," *Herald* (Everett, WA), October 23, 2008, http://www.heraldnet.com/article/20081023/ NEWS01/710239912 (accessed August 21, 2013).

3. "EBSCO Publishing," *Wikipedia*, http://en.wikipedia.org/wiki/EBSCO_Publishing (accessed January 2, 2013); and "Goodreads Partners with EBSCO: Reader Reviews Now Available to Libraries," *GoodReads.com*, June 22, 2011. http://www.goodreads.com/blog/show/286-goodreads -partners-with-ebsco-reader-reviews-now-available-to-libraries (accessed January 2, 2013).

4. "Illinois Volunteer librarians Create Statewide Information Portal," *Library Journal*, May 26, 2004, http://lj.libraryjournal.com/2004/05/ljarchives/illinois-volunteer-librarians -create-statewide-information-portal/ (accessed July 4, 2011).

5. Poster from Indianapolis–Marion County Public Library, http://www.imcpl.org/events/ srp2010/rgiants.php (accessed January 3, 2013). Read about how this program works in Katharine L. Kan, *Sizzling Summer Reading Programs*, 2nd ed. (Chicago: ALA Editions, 2006), 85.

6. London (Ontario) Public Library, "One-on-One English Conversation Mentor," http:// www.londonpubliclibrary.ca/conversationcircleapplicationform (accessed March 31, 2013).

7. Pam Highsmith, "Talk Time: A Library Volunteer's Perspective," *Texas Library Journal* 82, no. 1 (Spring 2006): 48.

8. "Literacy Tutors Are Volunteers," Newport Beach, http://www.newportbeachlibrary.org/ literacy/volunteers (accessed September 27, 2008).

9. Jeanette Larson, "Building a Culture of Literacy through Día: Library Events Celebrate Bilingual Bookjoy," *American Libraries*, March 22, 2011, http://americanlibrariesmagazine.org/ features/01132011/building-culture-literacy-through-d (accessed July 1, 2011).

10. Virginia Rankin, "Strength in Numbers: Struggling Kids Benefit from Volunteer Tutors," *School Library Journal*, January 1, 2006, http://www.libraryjournal.com/slj/printissuecurrentissue/ 864177-427/strength_in_numbers.html.csp (accessed July 4, 2011).

11. Lauren Barack, "Are There Any Volunteers? A Pain-Free Approach to Getting the Very Best out of Parents," *School Library Journal*, December 1, 2010, http://www.schoollibraryjournal.com/ slj/mobilemhome/887721-461/are_there_any_volunteers_a.html.csp (accessed July 4, 2011).

12. Loriene Roy, Trina Bolfing, and Bonnie Brzozowski, "Computer Classes for Job Seekers: LIS Students Team with Public Librarians to Extend Public Services," *Public Library Quarterly* 29, no. 3 (2010): 193–209.

13. http://www.bpef-online.org/volunteer/volunteers/volunteer-opportunities/ (accessed January 19, 2013).

14. Kay Shelton, "Starting a Volunteer Program in a Community College Library," *Community and Junior College Libraries* 14, no. 3 (2008): 161–77. This article was downloaded from the University of Washington Libraries, February 3, 2011.

15. Maine Is Technology website, http://www.maine.gov/newsletter/backissues/apr99/computers_for_schools_and_librar.htm (accessed January 19, 2013).

16. *Staying Connected: A Toolkit to Build Support in the Community for Your Technology Programs* (Seattle, WA: Bill & Melinda Gates Foundation, 2002), chap. 5, 31–38, http://www.webjunction.org/content/dam/WebJunction/Documents/webjunction/Staying-Connected-Toolkit-Chapters-1-7.pdf (accessed April 13, 2007).

17. Salina (KS) Public Library, "Library Success: A Best Practices Wiki," http://www.salpublib.org/Class/schedule.htm (accessed April 13, 2011).

18. "Volunteer Speed Matching at the Library," *Public Libraries* 47, no. 2 (March–April 2008): 14–15.

19. Reported on the ALTAFF website, n.d., http://www.ala.org/ala/mgrps/divs/altaff/friends/ideasharing/volunteers.cfm (accessed December 20, 2009).

20. http://www.sjlibrary.org/about/locations/king/lawyers.htm (accessed April 13, 2012).

21. Elizabeth Schobernd, Toni Tucker, and Sharon Wetzel, "Closing the Gap: Use of Student Volunteers in an Academic Library," *Technical Services Quarterly* 26, no. 3 (2009): 194–98.

22. Meg Dedolph, "Help Wanted: Bookkeeping; Libraries Need Volunteers for Summer Duty," *Naperville* (IL) *Sun*, April 30, 2004, retrieved from HighBeam Research at http://www.highbeam.com (accessed December 24, 2009).

23. Katherine "Kit" Willis, "Adopt-a-Dewey," *Public Library Quarterly* 19, no. 1 (May 2001): 13–17.

24. Albi Calman, "Are Volunteers Worth the Effort? Maximizing the Value of Volunteers in the Hospital Library," *Journal of Hospital Librarianship* 10, no. 4 (October 2010): 395–401.

25. Virginia A. Lingle, "Volunteers in the Medical Library: Issues and Suggestions for Their Use," *Medical Reference Services Quarterly* 3, no. 4 (November 1984): 45–56.

26. "ALA Volunteers to Aid 22 New Orleans Libraries, Schools, Colleges, Community Organizations during Annual Conference," posted May 16, 2006, http://www.ala.org/news/news/pressreleases2006/may2006/alavol06 (accessed January 9, 2007).

27. "NOAH: New York Online Access to Health—NOAH." healthfinder.gov, http://www.health.gov/nhic/NHICScripts/Entry.cfm?HRCode=HR2893 (accessed April 12, 2013).

28. The site is http://radicalreference.info/.

29. Shinjoung Yeo, Joel J. Rane, James R. Jacobs, Lia Friedman, and Jenna Freedman, "Radical Reference: Taking Information to the Street (Viewpoint)," *Information Outlook* 9, no. 6 (June 2005): 55–57. The organization's mission statement and a report on some of its activities is at http://radicalreference.info/about.

30. "2012 Book Fair Information: The 28th Annual Newberry Library Book Fair, July 25 to July 29, 2012," http://www.newberry.org/sites/default/files/textpage-attachments/2012BookFairVolunteerHandbook.pdf (accessed April 1, 2013).

31. Mary Wyly, "Uncommon Human Resources: The Newberry Library Volunteer Program," *Library Trends* 41, no. 2 (Fall 1992): 316–29.

32. Renee Olson, "Internet Public Library Debuts on the WWW," *School Library Journal* 41, no. 5 (May 1995): 14–16; Beverly Goldberg, "Virtual Patrons Flock into the Internet Public Library," *American Libraries* 26, no. 5 (May 1995): 387–88; "About ipl2," http://www.ipl.org/div/about/ (accessed April 18, 2013).

33. Ann B. Beecher, "Wayfinding Tools in Public Library Buildings: A Multiple Case Study" (PhD diss., University of North Texas, May 2004), borrowed from Indiana University, Bloomington. Available from ProQuest.

34. Susan J. Ellis, "Volunteering in Pajamas and Other Joys of Online Service Programs: Executive Update," March 2004, http://www.asaecenter.org/Resources/EUArticle.cfm?ItemNumber=11638 (accessed April 1, 2013). One report on SLPL focus groups is Glen E. Holt, "As Parents and Teachers See It: The Community Values of a Public Library," *The Bottom Line* 10, no. 1 (1997): 32–35.

4

Planning

PRACTICAL QUESTIONS

Creating a successful library volunteer program is not as hard as sending a rocket to the moon or as complicated as explaining the implication of Einstein's equation, $E = mc^2$. Neither is successful volunteerism so easily accomplished that it takes no more effort than what Judy Garland and Mickey Rooney needed to "put on a show" in one of their 1930s Hollywood musicals.

Balancing the two realities of a naive simplicity and atomic complexity, successful volunteerism in a library always involves some basic steps. In the following section, you'll find an overview of those steps that will help you lay out what you need to do to start or to reform a volunteer program and evaluation techniques that will help you measure results. The process involves both basic, practical questions and strategic planning.

The list of questions that follows is designed to help you with your volunteer program planning. It is derived both from experience and a summary of considerable "how-to" volunteer literature. In that literature, Anna Mills, a school librarian and technologist at Eaton Middle School in Eaton, Colorado, concludes, "For any volunteer project to be successful, your library must have the ability to manage the project. That means you must be able to define the project in a clear, realistic way; write a scope of work for yourselves and the volunteer; evaluate the skills of the volunteer against the scope; [and] have the capacity to supervise and evaluate the volunteer's work."[1]

Using Mills's characterization as a starting point, we have devised the following basic task assignments for moving volunteer projects ahead. We recommend you review and answer the questions as part of your planning process before embarking on a new or renewed volunteer program whether your library is rich or poor, little or big, basic or specialized in its constituency

1. Can You Define a Needed Volunteer Project in a Clear and Realistic Way?

The answer to this question is as simple as the task is complex. Everything in every library ought to find its rationale in the organization's institutional mission and vision. At St. Louis Public Library (SLPL), where both authors worked for more than a decade, the institutional mission was to use library materials and services "to improve the quality of individual, family and community life." The key word in the SLPL mission statement is "improve." Improvement can be accomplished only by proactive change. And the best and the easiest proactive changes occur when a library's leaders and managers begin with a clear goal that has specific objectives.

So, what change do you want to make in your library services—and can volunteers help?

- For example, the improvement of early childhood literacy is something that librarians often state as a goal. How can volunteers play a role in this improvement program? Do you want to improve this situation within your community or at your school? Is early literacy part of your mission?
- Or, if students (elementary, high school, college) need tutoring in the evening, what, if anything, should the library do to improve that situation for its community? How can volunteers help? Is tutoring at the library mission-driven?
- Or, if your users and potential users are starved for certain kinds of intellectual and artistic activity, what, if anything, can volunteers do to help your library improve that situation? Is this kind of programming part of your library's mission?

2. What Time Commitment Does the Project Require?[2]

Mills's preceding query offers different ways of dealing with one of the library world's principal problems—i.e., the issue of time. Is the proposed project something that has to be done right now, as, for example, a funded summer outreach program to day-care centers? Is the proposed project short-term or ongoing? Using volunteer researchers to aid scientists at their projects can be accomplished quickly or last for decades. Another time-related question concerns your willingness to define the scope or the terms of what has to be accomplished to declare the goal as having been met. The last time question is specifically about the time duration of the proposed project.

3. Is Volunteerism the Best Way to Deal with the Problem You Want to Solve? The Least Bad Way? The Only Way?

Libraries historically solve their problems in three ways:

- Adding staff who will be charged with solving the problem.
- Hiring a consultant who will be paid to articulate a solution to the problem.
- Adding a small or a large cadre of volunteers who are asked (or charged) with solving the problem.

If a volunteer program is listless or troubled, start with basics: "Why does it exist at all?" Other decisions will flow from the answer to that question. If you are starting a volunteer program, begin with its rationale: Why is it needed? Asking library volunteers to clean the library restroom may be helpful and you may find a volunteer to do it, but how does this activity help the library? Good use of volunteer time should help the library achieve its mission.

Answering this question should help you define an optimal (or at least an expedient) solution to your stated community problem. Volunteerism is only *one* possible solution. It is not the only solution, and it is not necessarily the best solution. Like all policies that deal with people, especially those working for or in an institution, volunteers have both pluses and minuses. It is up to library leaders who make institutional policy and budgeting decisions to determine if the project has time and cost merit—or, if volunteers provide an effective solution.

4. What Kind of Volunteers Do You Need?

The rationale for volunteer programs is to accomplish specific work tasks, to develop a group of people who know about the library and support it, and to better serve the library's users. If you already have a volunteer program, are participants the kind of volunteers you need to make it successful? Here are some basic questions to answer as part of your planning.

- What are the minimal requirements for a volunteer? (Age, literacy level, language skills, physical capabilities, etc.)
- Is there a residency requirement or a residency preference for volunteers? From your constituency? Outside your geographic focus?
- What record keeping do you need to do to keep track of your volunteers?
- Is a background check required before a volunteer is assigned work? What is checked?
- How many volunteers can you manage effectively?
- Do you have volunteer job descriptions that include how many hours will it take to do the anticipated task(s)? This estimate is especially needed if the anticipated volunteer tasks are large or complex.

Most libraries have several types of volunteers. Schools generally employ parents, students, and community members as volunteers. Universities may have faculty, students, or alums. Public libraries have young people, older people, court-ordered people, church people, and civic club people, just to name a few. Getting the right people with the right skills is crucial to volunteer success. Not all volunteers come with the skills and knowledge they need, so training is important, as is assessing each volunteer and assigning them to tasks they can do and enjoy.

Deciding what kind of volunteers you need leads naturally to the next question.

5. What Kind of Orientation and Training Will Volunteers Need?

Specifically, what will volunteers need to help improve the library's services and products and to feel successful and positive about their volunteer assignments?

6. What Is Your Potential Budget? If the Budget Is Tight or Nonexistent, What Changes or Cuts Will Be Made in Current Operations to Obtain the Project Budget? How Can You Raise Funds?

Once you have identified the task that needs to be done or the problem that needs to be solved, and that the best solution is volunteers; you must answer questions about resources. Lots of people, especially many elected and university officials looking for cheap solutions, advance the concept of "volunteers to replace staff" as a bright way out of a library's financial problems. They see volunteers as an easy choice, because implicitly it appears cheaper than any other solution.

That view of organization—especially a helping organization like a library—is incredibly simplistic and unrealistic. That's because volunteers are not free. Anyone who has ever watched a skilled reference librarian combine knowledge of paper and electronic sources to come up with "the right answer" recognizes that training and experience bring huge advantages in selecting the best article, book, or database from which to derive the best and/or quickest answer to a library user trying to answer some question. To train volunteers to replace or supplement a reference librarian will certainly have costs associated with them. And, to opt not to train the volunteers who are asked to do these tasks has even larger costs. (See Chapter 6 for more about costs of volunteers.)

Where will the resources come from to obtain the appropriate skills, provide the appropriate training, recruit the appropriate volunteers, and supervise the appropriate volunteer work to make sure that an assigned volunteer task gets done on time and within budget—and that the results of the project are appropriately linked into the work requirements of other appropriate staff? Such questions are not philosophical; they are organizational, and without answering them, your volunteer program is bound to have more trouble than it needs to.

7. How Will You Connect the Library's Volunteer Program into the Other Parts of the Organization to Ensure Good Communication and Access to Resources?

As much as and perhaps more than any other program, a volunteer program must have access to administration, multiple service points, facilities, operations, finance—and potential connections to other organizations as well. This is more challenging than staff communications, as volunteers spend far less time at the library than staff and are less sophisticated than staff about library operations. They often don't know who to ask if they have a question or a problem.

8. What Skills and Attitudes Do You Want the Manager of Volunteers to Have?

- What should be the requirements of the volunteer manager's job description?
- Is this a part-time job, or is managing volunteers assigned to an already established position (e.g., assistant director, marketing manager, or department head)?

- To whom should that manager report?
- And, what are the initiative-making authorities built into the volunteer director's office?

How volunteers are managed will vary. This can depend on how volunteering has been done in the past, what government agencies do or don't do to support volunteers, and what other nonprofits use and share volunteers. A good place to examine these differences is in the reports of the Corporation for National and Community Service, which you can find on the Internet.[3]

MANAGEMENT DECISIONS

Once you have answers to the questions above, you can create a volunteer plan based on what you have decided. You know which projects volunteers will do, how many volunteers you need, what skills volunteers will have, and what training you will need to provide. You will have a supervisor or leader for your volunteer program as well as a budget for the program.

Based on this plan, you need to be specific about how your volunteer program will work. The decisions you make will form the foundation of a successful volunteer program. For smaller libraries or libraries that have only a few things for volunteers to do, each of these decisions can be fairly simple. But every volunteer program leader should have specific ways to carry out the volunteer plan, no matter what the size of the program.

A Job Description for Each Type of Volunteer Task

This description can be a list, but it is more helpful if it specifies what needs to be done, how long it will take, what skills are needed, and which staff person is the contact for the volunteer. In large systems, a full description ensures consistency from department to department as well as from staff supervisor to staff supervisor.

Recruitment: How Are Volunteers Recruited?

- What communication tools are used in the recruitment of volunteers (flyers, announcements, volunteer events, social media postings, newspaper ads, etc.)?
- Does the library's application help match potential volunteers to specific jobs?
- Are volunteers recruited by cooperation with other organizations? Who and how, if this is the case? Is this relationship stable? Or, in flux?

Orientation and Training: What Orientation and Training Do Your Volunteers Receive?

- Introduction to the library, staff, and library rules.
- Job skills—what does the volunteer need to know how to do?
- Communication—how do volunteers communicate with their supervisor or administration?
- Help understanding the work expectations of the volunteer task?

Retention: How Long Do Volunteers Stay? Do You Want Them to Stay Longer or Shorter?

- What is the average length of time commitment? Is there a minimal time commitment?
- What would make volunteers stay longer?
- How do you work with short-term volunteers (workday or service requirements)?

Benefits: What Benefits Do Volunteers Get?

- Learn new skills, meet new people.
- Work experience.
- Staff recognition as valuable contributors.
- Thank you parties, awards, gifts.
- Publicity in some form?
- Special events with well-known authors or local personalities.
- Recommendations or a record of time worked, jobs done.

Benefits: What Does the Library Get?

- Donated work completed (can be listed as a dollar amount donation).
- Access to specialized or added skills.
- Positive contact with the public.
- Volunteers act as ambassadors for the library in the community, school, or university.

Lastly, any library needs to know how it will manage the volunteer program. While some volunteers are skilled and experienced enough to work on their own, most volunteers need to be supervised and have contact with staff each time they volunteer. As indicated elsewhere in this book, different programs require varying supervision levels. In small libraries, the librarian is likely to be in charge of the volunteer program; in larger libraries, there will be a volunteer manager who reports to someone at the directorial level. Schools or universities may have a volunteer program run for all parts of the organization with the library being one choice among many for volunteers. In this case the library should have a contact person who is in touch with the school or university volunteer department as well as the person who directs the volunteers in the library. However it is accomplished, volunteers need to be supervised, and the volunteer program needs to be coordinated.

Volunteer supervision includes explaining what needs to be done, reinforcing library rules and practices, giving positive reinforcement, correcting mistakes, and exchanging pleasantries.[4] Volunteers need all or some of this supervision every time they work at the library, so the time and patience library staff have to supervise may limit the number of volunteers your library can manage.

In order to avoid confusion, a staff member has to coordinate all aspects of the volunteer program. More on staff leadership for the volunteer program follows.

EXERCISE CAUTION IN VOLUNTEER ASSIGNMENT

As shown in Chapters 2 and 3, volunteers do well at many different kinds of library tasks. But there are limits to what volunteers should be asked to do. Every library administrator needs to be cautious, particularly about replacement of paid, skilled staff with volunteers.

That is true even when the economy goes sour, and libraries are looking everywhere for more money—and more staff. Through the last century, with each downtown in this nation's economy, someone has proposed that an army of unpaid volunteers can do most any job just as well as highly trained and often well-paid professionals in medicine, law, firefighting, national security, local security, housekeeping, and information gathering and interpretation. Most recently, because of the Great Recession of 2007–2009, many libraries have struggled to deliver a modicum of their former services.[5] In the process, to quote a headline from Helena, Montana, "Library Plugs into Volunteer Power."[6] Often, this new volunteer power fizzles out, and, as soon as the recovery comes, paid professional staff are rehired, with established quality standards put in place.[7] Careful thought and decision making about volunteers always should precede their installation.

The Australian Library and Information Association ends its excellent statement of principle about the deskilling of professional library work with volunteers serving as replacements by noting, "The replacement of trained, paid library staff by volunteers can only lead to a deterioration in the standard and the effectiveness of services, be wasteful of resources and be detrimental to the interests of library users."[8]

To rely on volunteerism for critical library work invites trouble with salaries, staff evaluations, and employment equity rules, whether staff is unionized or not. Here are some examples of volunteer assignments that have institutional trouble built into them.

- *Privacy issues*: Volunteers check out materials for card holders in a library within a state that has strong laws protecting library user privacy. Check on your state laws in regard to privacy of library records. Assigning volunteers to check out without appropriate legal limits being explained to the volunteers recording the transactions may cause a problem.
- *Financial issues*: This applies to fund-raising of all kinds. If friends or volunteers use the library's name to raise or earn funds, then the library has a liability connected with that activity. That probably holds true, for example, even if all or almost all of the books and electronic items sold come from public donations, and not from the public's collections. Establish an audit trail and stick to it.
- *Workplace safety issues*: A middle-aged volunteer complains about back pain after moving boxes in preparation for the university library book sale. No one mentioned the need to take care in "lifting loaded book boxes" or gave any training on the weight limits and how to pick up and put down loaded boxes to the volunteers before this activity started. Here is a liability suit waiting to happen.
- *Reliability*: A group from the local senior center volunteers to organize a preschool story-time. They are successful in getting children to attend and the first session is excellent.

At the second session, library staff have to fill in at the last minute because one volunteer was a no-show. The third and fourth sessions have to be canceled because the seniors had schedule conflicts. A public relations debacle is just around the corner.

Conflict of Interest

Depending on the recruitment that your library has undertaken, the conflict-of-interest issue could play a significant role. Conflict of interest should be part of your recruitment effort so you establish availability before a potential volunteer starts at the library. Attorneys, financial organization staff, and other businesses—including other not-for-profit executives—may find conflict-of-interest issues in some kinds of volunteer work they might undertake for your library. Where to invest money, prior legal commitment to a different client, the engagement in the sale of personal services, etc., all may raise the conflict-of-interest flag. The way that libraries handle conflict of interest is by having a general conflict-of-interest policy and asking those who recognize they have such a conflict to take appropriate action when a particular issue appears. Because this issue often involves legal controversy, there are many different conflict-of-interest statements on the Internet. One of the most detailed is for volunteers of the United States Tennis Association, which covers a whole range of potential conflicts.[9] ALA is at the other end of the conflict-of-interest spectrum. Its draft statement for libraries is less than one page.[10]

Even if you are certain that conflict of interest will never rear its ugly head in your library, this policy is a good one to have on hand with an established official position so that when the issue arises with volunteers or staff, your institution is not embarrassed by it. The message here is to think ahead to what types of things might go wrong, and plan accordingly.

Just as there are some library work activities in which you might not want volunteers involved, there may be library volunteer programs already operating that should be left alone. If, for example, a community computer club already is doing an excellent job of providing instruction to new computer users, leave it alone. The old adage, "If it ain't broke, don't fix it!" applies to lots of volunteer issues. But, if the Friends annual book sale is making a lot less money than in former years, then it makes sense to explore what is wrong and make changes. Don't expect a new group of volunteers to improve some troubled volunteer operation without changes in training, expectation, supervision, and compliance with library policies.

Before making changes in volunteer programs, consider what's working and what's not working, and figure out why.

VOLUNTEER POSITION DESCRIPTIONS

In our own experience, we at times wanted to recruit a volunteer expert financial consultant, a dozen persons who would help us put out mailings to regular and special constituent groups, and summer-reading-club outreach volunteers who could travel to different day-care centers and schools to talk with classes and meeting groups about what they could get out of summer reading. The latter group of volunteers had to be able to tell stories as well.

The variety of needs in this paragraph is a simplistic reflection of all the different jobs that libraries want volunteers to do. Our advice in handling such activity is always the same: Think and define before you act. There are lots of good examples of volunteer job descriptions. In general, however, volunteer job descriptions should be no longer than necessary, balancing what a library needs and what must be said to attract good recruits.

Your first action in volunteer recruitment is to define the work that you need volunteers to do. That's really not hard, especially if you already have job descriptions written for any of your staff. Your volunteer job positions can be defined exactly the same way using the same kind of language and about the same amount of detail. If you don't have job descriptions or volunteer descriptions handy as a model, go to the Internet and look at Susan Ellis's general but useful "Worksheet for Writing a Volunteer Description" (2002).[11] Another document with the same purpose is Joanne Fritz's "How to Write a Volunteer Position Description."[12] We also like the "Sample Technology Volunteer Job Description" for a Main Library Cyber Center Attendant at Arlington (Virginia) Public Library (2006).[13] The extensive job descriptions for volunteer administrators in the Appendix on King County cover all the bases for large libraries.

The required points of a job description are that it should include a name or title of the activity, a brief description of what the job entails, a list of skills or knowledge needed to do the job, and what time commitment is needed. The job description should be realistic for volunteers and should be interesting or attractive to the volunteers at your library. Peter Drucker asserts, "People require clear assignments. They need to know what the institution expects of them. ... Everyone in the non-profit institution, whether chief executive or volunteer foot soldier, needs first to think through his or her own assignment. '*What should this institution hold me accountable for?*' "[14]

Be sensitive to a final issue about job descriptions: "Simple job descriptions" often become legal documents when disputes erupt over working rules and behavior.

LEADERSHIP FOR THE VOLUNTEER PROGRAM

With the exception of the library CEO, no single library position needs more firm leadership/management than the person in charge of volunteers. The more independent the volunteer group is from the regular administrative framework of the library, the greater the need for someone who actually knows how to lead/manage people, both within the organization and as part of partnering with other organizations.

The reason for the difficulty in finding an appropriate person for volunteer leader is because of the variety of management tasks with which that person has to deal and the extent of the competencies that such a person must have to do a good job. As stated previously, in small libraries the volunteer "leader" is the person who is head of the library. Friends groups are often led by a volunteer—a Friend elected to lead by the group. Some larger libraries can hire a full- or part-time staff person to lead and manage the volunteers. (See Chapter 7 for much more information on Friends.)

Energize on the Internet publishes a convenient list of knowledge areas that a well-prepared volunteer leader might have. Obviously, if the volunteer program is large, requiring more than one staff member to watch over it, these variant knowledge areas could be in staff other than the director.[15] We have added some items to this list on behalf of libraries generally.

- Bookstore, library store, or retail experience
- Communication and collaboration within organizations, and with individual volunteers and staff
- Delegation
- Diversity
- Employee/volunteer relations
- Ethics
- Evaluation
- Event planning
- Financial planning and management; fundraising
- Legal issues
- Marketing
- Motivation
- Policy development
- Recognition
- Record keeping
- Recruitment
- Retention
- Risk and liability
- Service learning
- Social networking
- Supervision
- Training
- Virtual volunteering[16]

Remember, volunteer manager's skill areas also are specified in the King County model in the Appendix.

Since many organizations emphasize competencies, here is a list of competencies written for volunteer managers in the State of Maine.

1. Articulate and commit to the organization's vision; connect vision to goals.
2. Partner, collaborate, work with others, and facilitate work groups.
3. Empower others.
4. Convert needs into objectives and action plans.
5. Learn, apply, and model the professional principles of volunteer management.[17]

You can also go online to see the competencies for the library volunteer coordinator from Marion County Public Library (headquartered in Ocala, Florida), which has a very accessible summary.[18]

No matter what it is called, a healthy volunteer program is one that is led by someone who has the skills identified by Energize, and knowledge of the library and librarianship, as well as the ability to demonstrate the leadership competencies identified by the state of Maine. While a smaller volunteer program might not attract a volunteer leader with all these characteristics, it is important to recognize that the best volunteer programs are those that are purposefully managed by a knowledgeable leader.

Performance Appraisal

One important piece of the job description of a volunteer manager is how that person will be evaluated. Sometimes writing the performance expectations is the best way to clarify what your program actually needs from your manager. Here is the example of an evaluation of a successful volunteer coordinator:

MANAGER OF VOLUNTEERS: PERFORMANCE APPRAISAL

Overall Performance:

Day-to-Day Operations
1. Volunteer office runs smoothly and volunteers are managed in an effective manner.
2. Improvement in being on time with reports and paperwork.

Communication and Teamwork
1. Effective in working and communication with a wide variety of staff.
2. Helpful in solving problems that involve volunteers.
3. Good coordination of book sales.

Public Service
1. Volunteer newsletter is begun.
2. Recruitment of volunteers of all types is successful. Can now expand to include members of the immigrant population.
3. Volunteer recognition is effective.

Leadership
1. Active membership in volunteer associations.
2. Helpful participation in special grant activities.
3. Strong advocate for volunteers within the library.

To sum up, our general experience with library volunteer leaders is that lots of them tend to be "nice," but not nearly knowledgeable enough for the work they are attempting to do. Volunteer management is a set of knowledge areas and management competencies that are not taught in any library school. If you really want a successful volunteer program, such an appointment needs to be considered carefully and thought through.

If this responsibility is thrust upon a willing library professional, there must be training—and probably lots of it—or your volunteer leader inevitably will take the program through a rocky period while she learns all the ins and outs of the job. The natural tendency is to turn inward for the volunteer head appointment—i.e., to turn to someone who "knows" how the organization operates. In such an appointment, however, the hiring issue should be the "new" areas of expertise that need to be brought into the organization—and the general management competencies that the volunteer leader needs. If you can afford only a new hire for your volunteer coordinator, you might look at new graduates from volunteer management programs, which very often are allied with university sociology departments or public administration programs.[19]

Objective evidence suggests that effective, visible management of your volunteers produces higher net benefits to the organization. Hager and Brundey write:

> Those organizations that have a coordinator who devotes substantial attention to volunteer administration are rewarded with high net benefits scores. In other briefs, we have referred to the adoption of volunteer management practices and the presence of a volunteer coordinator as the two major dimensions of "volunteer management capacity." In sum, organizations that invest in volunteer management capacity are more likely to attain high net benefits.[20]

Finally, the two authors conclude that smaller charities are a bit more successful in realizing net benefits generally [and] achieve higher net benefits than the largest ones.[21] This fact should hearten libraries that are neither huge nor even quite large. The best library volunteer coordinators we know were hired from the directorship of a university volunteer program, the regional office of the United Way and from a housekeeping position for a large local church, which used huge numbers of volunteers with a few paid line leaders. Where to start such a search? Look at the e-page compilation of Rebecca Nelles.[22]

STAFF AND VOLUNTEERS

As well as having solid leadership for your volunteer program, it is essential to have staff cooperation in branches or work units when volunteers appear to undertake assignments. Without staff support, volunteers are unlikely to succeed or find volunteering at the library enjoyable. The cold reality is that some staff will see volunteers almost entirely as persons willing to do for no salary what currently salaried staff are getting paid to do.

That idea of volunteers as substitutes for paid workers has been discussed hotly in library journals since the beginning of the Great Recession. For union leaders or worker advocates, volunteers often equate—or can be made to equate—to fewer paid job opportunities and even less control over working conditions. Sometimes the desire for control comes from fear. Fear of *change*, of the unknown, of *doing things differently*, of a situation not created by us, of *taking risks*. It is human nature to fear these things; it's how we've survived. So is adaptation; and times are changing, just as they always do, and we need to adapt.[23]

The best way to introduce volunteerism in a library policy discussion is to do it openly. Smart library administrators recognize that discussions about volunteers are going to provoke fears of loss of control, loss of jobs, and "loss of my salary." In a troubled library, the introduction or advancement of volunteers will be perceived by many staff as something leading to possible losses. Our best advice is to be ready for the issues and to get on top of such issues before they are raised. There is a wrong way to deal with such issues—namely, to ignore them or to let the volunteers work them out.

Given the significance of job and working condition control in libraries, what is the best way to manage the successful introduction and operation of volunteers into any library, no matter how specialized or how large or small? All protestations to the contrary, libraries mostly function as bureaucracies, either separately or in association with even larger bureaucracies such as schools, universities, and government agencies. Within this context, the principal problem is conflict avoidance—that is, the creation of a rule or a form or a procedure or a policy that will make more paperwork but slow volunteers and staff down when they have to maneuver through it and the procedures it invokes.

The whole point of a volunteer program is to recruit low-cost assistance to do work that needs to be accomplished to help the library move forward. Yet, volunteer management texts are full of bureaucratic tactics and forms to "fit" volunteers into the skein of library operations. Driggers and Dumas offer a whole section (11 pages) on "Volunteer Records," and there are forms to be used with volunteers inserted into nearly half of the other 34 chapters.[24] The thesis seems to be that volunteer documents of various kinds must match up with the bureaucracy of the most bureaucratic libraries.

By intent, this book is short on forms. The Internet is full of forms that can be used by librarians who want a form for any purpose in their volunteer program. In addition, most librarians are expert at creating forms. Forms, however, are not ends, but tools. Paper forms and rules should not drive programs; they record and furnish important information and give guidance that helps human beings do a good job at their tasks of monitoring or outlining the requirements for success in programs—including volunteers.

Finding and maintaining the balance of a library volunteer program is no easy process. Helping staff feel comfortable with volunteers so that control issues are reasonably handled is a significant key to success. In the best situation, staff welcome volunteers because they help the staff do their jobs and often free staff from some routine tasks

STAFF TRAINING

Consider how King County Library System administrators handled potential conflict over changes in the volunteers program (see the Appendix). The library's leaders credited the library's need to change the volunteers program to staff, took many of their suggestions on adoption, and, as you'll see in Chapter 8, set up a new electronic information system to inform staff about what was happening in the volunteer program.

Even without this sophisticated approach, a great way to make staff comfortable with volunteers is through training. Any staff person who supervises a volunteer should at the least have an orientation to the volunteer program, so they understand what the volunteers should be doing and are acquainted with the rules and procedures of the volunteer program. Even creating a brief guideline for supervising volunteers or a checklist will make staff feel more comfortable and competent.[25] A sample checklist follows.

STAFF GUIDE TO MANAGING VOLUNTEERS

Welcome
    Greet volunteer by name
    Activities of the day
    Have a secure place for coats, purse, and other personal belongings
    Thank volunteer for service

Volunteer Orientation
    Tour of library or department (including restroom and staff lounge)
    Introduce other staff and volunteers
    Explain mission of library and overview of services (in Volunteer Handbook)
    Explain key rules and procedures (in Volunteer Handbook)
    Confirm when volunteer will work
    How to communicate e-mail addresses and phone numbers, how to find you in person

Job Training
    Confirm what job or task the volunteer expects to do
    Review written instructions for each task the volunteer does
    Answer volunteer's questions
    Demonstrate how to do the task
    Watch volunteer practice task
    Check on volunteer's progress, answer volunteer questions

Supervision
    Keep track of hours served, compile monthly, and send to volunteer coordinator
    Correct errors pleasantly, praise success
    Discipline in private
    Ask for help from volunteer coordinator if problems are not resolved
    Answer questions, ask for suggestions from volunteers when appropriate
    Participate in volunteer recognition events

Obviously each library will have differing lists depending on the size of the library, staff structure, and the volunteers themselves. Even the most reliable volunteers need to know about changes at the library and have regular, useful, and pleasant interaction with staff every time they help the library.

For library staff who need to learn more about managing their volunteer program, there are several sources of continuing education. United Way or other local service organizations often offer workshops on topics of interest to library volunteer managers. The state library or local university may offer workshops or courses about managing volunteers. The Council for Certification in Volunteer Administration offers individuals certification in volunteer administration through study, portfolios, and examination.[26] Energize, Inc., lists about 40 degree or certification programs in volunteer administration located in the United States and Canada.[27] Many of these programs are part of a public administration program but might allow auditing or nondegree students to take classes.

COMMUNITY HELP WITH MANAGING VOLUNTEERS

There is no need to operate your volunteer program in a vacuum. You can find help from a variety of sources.

Community Agencies

Is the United Way active in your community? Is there a charitable agency like the United Way that can help you with recruitment, or do you have to do it alone? Not surprisingly, community organizations like United Way, the Junior League, university volunteer offices or local education foundations, and agencies like the state library can be called on for advice about how to improve your volunteer program. Local United Ways often host a Volunteer Administrator's Network or VAN. VANs hold meetings and facilitate cooperation and coordination among volunteer coordinators in a geographic location. Or, as a group called Association of Volunteer Professionals of Midland, Texas, states, "we meet once a month to celebrate our success, investigate new ideas and concepts, and share a little lunch."[28] The library will find this group as a source of information on volunteers and a way to build partnerships with other agencies. LLAMA and ASCLA, as well as many ALA divisions, have resources for volunteer management as well as contact with others who manage library volunteers.

Other Libraries

Of course, you should also look to other libraries. Which ones are recognized as operating exemplary volunteer programs? Does your state library or library system keep track of volunteer programs in your area? There may be libraries that serve similar schools or communities outside your region with volunteer programs that would be models for your volunteers. Net searches or contacts at professional conferences can help you find the answers to your volunteer questions.

Your Own Staff and Volunteers

Your institution might also want to do what King County Library System did (Appendix), conducting a survey of its staff to get help on what was needed, how to organize, and implementation options. One item we picked up in our own informal survey of staff in St. Louis concerned younger siblings—i.e., "The kids who attend our after-school programs bring along their little brothers and sisters who cause disturbances because there is nothing for them to do and all staff already are very busy." We then organized volunteers to play games and read to these younger children. It is also worthwhile to ask volunteers for ideas to improve the program. You can do this through a survey, interviews, or focus groups.

In addition to occasional advice from staff or volunteers, you may want to build in a mechanism for ongoing involvement in management of your volunteer program. Being "left out" of communication about volunteers can sour lots of staff on volunteers. Whether "regular communication" within the organization is by paper, e-mail, or intranet, it is important to encourage interaction between staff and the volunteer manager. Above all, remember that it is management's role to bring improvements in library volunteerism with the least discomfort to regular staff.[29] Some libraries have a committee of volunteers, who help plan activities and who can give feedback as issues arise. Often the Friends board may serve as a sounding board on volunteer issues.

Adroit implementation of your volunteer program can make all the difference in the world. It ensures that you are mission driven, are efficient, and will get the most possible out of your volunteers, and that the volunteers will have a positive experience. But beware—planning is not an end; doing well is the end. Most libraries can set up simple procedures, follow them, evaluate them, and change them as needed. Implementation strategies should be as simple as possible and let you spend most of your effort with your volunteers and most of your volunteers' efforts on helping the library.

NOTES

1. Anna Mills, "Volunteer, Consultant or Staff: A Guide to Determining How to Staff for a Technical Project," *WebJunction*, 432310, http://www.webjunction.org/documents/webjunction/Volunteer_Consultant_or_Staff.html (accessed June 23, 2013).

2. Ibid.

3. Corporation for National and Community Service (CNCS). http://www.nationalservice.gov/.

4. Preston Driggers and Eileen Dumas, *Managing Library Volunteers*, 2nd ed. (Chicago: American Library Association, 2011), 56.

5. Hannah's Treasure Chest, "Nonprofits are in Trouble, Volunteers Can Help," posted May 19, 2009, http://www.facebook.com/note.php?note_id=83596572049 (accessed May 30, 2011).

6. "Library Plugs into Volunteer Power," *St. Helena Star*, April 23, 2009, http://napavalleyregister.com/star/lifestyles/library-plugs-into-volunteer-power/article_19b4a76d-8641-57b0-98f8-1878f3890a7e.html (accessed July 10, 2010).

7. Susan J. Ellis, "Replacing Volunteers with Paid Staff," Energize, September 2008, http://www.energizeinc.com/hot/2008/08sep.html (accessed January 6, 2013).

8. Australian Library and Information Service, "Statement on Voluntary Work in Voluntary and Information Services" (adopted 2001, amended 2009), http://www.alia.org.au/about-alia/policies-standards-and-guidelines/statement-voluntary-work-library-and-information-services (accessed March 20, 2013).

9. United States Tennis Association, "Sample of Conflict of Interest and Disclosure Policy and Form," http://assets.usta.com/assets/1/15/CTA_Guide_-_Appendix_D.pdf (accessed December 12, 2012).

10. ALA, "Sample Board of Trustees and Library Employee Conflict of Interest Policy," http://www.ala.org/united/files/trustees/orgtools/policies/conflict-interest.doc (accessed May 11, 2013).

11. Susan Ellis, "Worksheet for Writing a Volunteer Description" (2002), http://www.oursharedresources.com/Resource/ViewResource/224 (accessed May 30, 2010).

12. Joanne Fritz, "How to Write a Volunteer Position Description," *About.com Guide*, http://nonprofit.about.com/od/volunteers/ht/voldespos.htm (accessed September 1, 2013).

13. Arlington (VA) Public Library, "Sample Technology Volunteer Job Description [for a Main Library Cyber Center Attendant]," http://www.co.arlington.va.us/lib/cyber/index.htm (accessed May 30, 2010).

14. Peter Drucker, *Managing the Non-Profit Organization: Principles and Practices* (New York: Harper-Business, 1992). See Chapter 5, "Summary: The Action Implications," especially page 184.

15. Energize. Volunteer Management Resource Library. Volunteer Management Skill Area. At http://www.energizeinc.com/art.html (accessed January 20, 2013).

16. Ibid.

17. Anne Schink and Lawrence Ullian, *Volunteer Management Competencies: Indicators for Novice to Expert* (Bangor: Maine Commission for Community Service/Edmund S. Muskie School of Public Service, 2007), http://muskie.usm.maine.edu/Publications/Volunteer MgmtCompetencies_Indicators.pdf (accessed May 9, 2013).

18. Marion County (FL) Board of County Commissioners, "Library Volunteer Program Coordinator [Job Description]," http://www.marioncountyfl.org/humanresources/HR_jobdesc/Library/LibraryVolunteerProgramCoordinator.pdf (accessed December 24, 2009).

19. Retrieved from Sociology Degree Programs, http://www.sociologydegreeprograms.org/social-work-careers/volunteer-coordinator/ (accessed November 12, 2012).

20. Mark A. Hager and Jeffrey L. Brudney, *Balancing Act: The Challenges and Benefits of Volunteers* (Washington, DC: Urban Institute, 2004), http://www.urban.org/UploadedPDF/411125_balancing_act.pdf (accessed May 27, 2009).

21. Ibid., 12.

22. Rebecca Nelles, "Things to Do to Become an Effective Volunteer Coordinator," http://www.ehow.com/list_6755482_things-become-effective-volunteer-coordinator.html (accessed November 12, 2012).

23. Bobbi Newman, "Control Is an Illusion You Need to Let Go," *Librarian by Day*, http://librarianbyday.net/2009/12/02/control-is-an-illusion-you-need-to-let-go/ (accessed April 23, 2012).

24. Driggers and Dumas, *Managing Library Volunteers*, 282–93.

25. Jean Pearlmutter and Paul Nelson, *Small Public Library Management* (Chicago: American Library Association, 2012), 39.

26. Council for Certification in Volunteer Administration website, http://www.cvacert.org/ (accessed May 13, 2013).

27. Energize, Inc. website, http://www.energizeinc.com/prof/class.html (accessed May 13, 2013).

28. Association of Volunteer Professionals website, http://www.avppb.org/index.html (accessed May 13, 2013).

29. Cathy Crosthwaite, "Library Volunteers: Management's Role in Eliminating Staff Resistance," electronic presentation on the California State Library Get Involved Website, http://getinvolvedca.org/resource/capacity-building-engaging-staff-and-unions/managements-role-eliminating-staff-resistance (accessed March 22, 2013).

5

Recruitment, Retention, and Recognition

A running joke among library directors about volunteer recruitment is, "All you have to do to get more volunteers is to build lots of new libraries." The basis of this little bit of acidic humor is a 2006 quote from then Chicago mayor Richard M. Daley, who noted: "Libraries today are community anchors. When we go out and dedicate a new library, it is amazing how many new volunteers we get from the community itself."[1]

Contrary to Daley's notion, volunteer recruitment should be timed so that it falls after the library has completed its volunteer program plan. These include legitimate, supervised volunteer workplaces, appropriate task descriptions, clear expectations, good supervision, and knowledge of the library's communications system can transmit appropriate information to, from, and about volunteers. If you haven't made the appropriate preparations to handle volunteers, your "volunteer troubles" will start immediately.

How and where will you recruit for volunteers? Are you going to recruit independently, through your regular communication channels like posters and counter pieces, via your social networking sites, through collaborations or partnerships with other agencies, on local or state websites, or through specialty organizations like faith-based agencies or corporations and private businesses? The latter question is basic: Your recruitment methods and style will largely determine the demographics and social values of the volunteers you attract.

So, what should a library volunteer recruitment program look and feel like?

MOTIVATIONS FOR VOLUNTEERING

An important part of recruitment is knowing what motivates volunteers to donate their work from their personal stores of free time.[2] There are lots of motivations to choose from—so many, in fact, that it is easy to get confused.[3] You can see the possibilities for that confusion if you peruse Volunteer Match's "incomplete list" of "20 Great Reasons to Volunteer." Their list includes helping others and contributing to a cause; making a difference and being productive; being involved with your community; developing new skills and meeting new people; expanding your horizons and getting out of the house; and that volunteering strengthens your resume and makes you feel better about yourself.[4]

National Bureau of Economic Research economist Richard Freeman in the mid-1990s found a good starting point when he termed volunteering "a 'conscience good or activity'—something that people feel morally obligated to do when asked, but which they would just as soon let someone else do."[5] The reality is that helping others makes lots of individuals happy.[6] That motivation type is "other-directed." Human beings, according to Nicholas Kristoff, are "hard wired" for this kind of social pleasure.[7]

The other type of motivation is "self-interested." Self-interest as much as other-directed motivations keep our service clubs, political parties, faith-based organizations, and secular charities staffed and funded. An appeal to the self-interest of potential volunteer recruits can be contained in three large categories.

- *Friendship*: Most libraries are basically friendly places, and working with friendly staff and other volunteers who share a new volunteer's interest in a neighborhood population (like new immigrants or particular groups of non-English-speakers), the successful organization of an event (e.g., helping organize a gala), or involvement with the development and delivery of successful service (e.g. story-telling to toddlers) is a great way to meet new people.
- *Social and Economic Advancement*: Library volunteering can build self-confidence in persons new to marketing themselves for a job, and the activity can provide valuable experience for future employment. People who want careers in libraries, teaching, or social work, for example, get valuable experience by volunteering in a library. Volunteer experience can also be extremely valuable for persons who have been out of the job market or for people with disabilities. The great variety of work tasks in a library often allows for demonstration and increase in skill levels for disabled persons, including mentally impaired and developmentally disabled. Such training is in line with a library's educational purpose and the intent of legislation that is part of mandating fair treatment for Americans with disabilities.
- *Improvement of Physical and Mental Health*: Volunteering also can be an aid to health. It is increasingly clear that seniors, for example, are healthier mentally and physically when they experience greater interaction with other people. The reality is that breaking social isolation to help others not only makes many happy; it also in many cases leads to good health.[8]

Many—even most—library volunteers begin with only a vague sense of how they might benefit from the experience. Chris Jarvis of Real Worth, a consulting firm that sets up volunteering programs for private-sector corporations, says that most people begin volunteering because of both extrinsic and intrinsic motivations.[9] That is, they volunteer because they want to help, and because they expect to get something out of it; but that latter element is mostly undefined when they enter the experience.

Jarvis writes, "If we remain motivated by exterior voices trying to convince us that we must help, or it is our duty, we will unfortunately remain personally detached from the work itself. In fact, extrinsic motivators such as rewards, incentives, or public recognition at a year-end celebration, may have a negative effect in the long run." When we find our intrinsic reasons in a volunteer task, it becomes our personal interest to do well at that job. In other words, motivating volunteers is accomplished the same way as motivating intrinsically motivated staff members. Volunteer Match, one of the most comprehensive volunteer sites on the Internet, assays this differentiation in volunteer goals this way:

> We can think of dozens of reasons why you should volunteer. Helping others and making a difference are just two. . . . Part of being a great volunteer is loving what you're doing. Find something that you're passionate about or something that inspires you, and then find a need in your community. There are dozens of reasons why you should volunteer—you just need to find the one that feels right.[10]

We believe it helps in recruitment if you regard motivations as evolutionary, even as the library self-consciously works to build the loyalty and the work acuity of the volunteer. Then volunteering becomes a process.

DETERRENTS TO VOLUNTEERING

In 2008, the Corporation for National and Community Services examined the attitudes of volunteers, nonvolunteers, and former volunteers trying to get at why some persons don't like to volunteer. Using a number of focus groups, CNCS in 2009 reported the following:

- *See Selves as Different*: "Non-volunteers see themselves as essentially different from volunteers. Non-volunteers tended to think of a volunteer as someone who was retired, without children in the home, and with lots of uncommitted time." Actually volunteer demographics are much broader.
- *Fear Time Commitment*: "Many non-volunteers fear the time commitment of service, expressing concerns that signing up for a volunteer activity would require that they continue indefinitely, even possibly for a lifetime."
- *More Willing if Trusted Friend Asks Them*: "Non-volunteers say that they are more likely to serve if a trusted friend asks them to serve. Some people are also more likely to serve if they are able to use a skill they already possess, and others are interested in learning something new. Interviewing potential volunteers to determine their interests in this regard can help ensure they get the experience they are looking for."[11]

VOLUNTEERING AS AN EXCHANGE

If you advance the idea that both volunteers and your organization win from the donated work experience, you can make the experience an exchange. Someone might volunteer by tutoring at the library and gain skill at helping one's own grandchildren at home. Or, by volunteering to review new books (or websites or music) on the library's website, the volunteer would get to read new materials without waiting on the reserves list. This notion of volunteerism is very useful in recruitment and in program planning. That way of thinking suggests that volunteers should benefit from their time with your library in the same way that your library benefits from their gift of time to do unpaid work.

The indefinite nature of motivations can be seen in the litany that Vancouver Public Library (Canada) uses to recruit teen volunteers. In their brief announcement for the TAG (Teen Advisory Group), the library recruits teens that will help develop teen program, write on the teen website, and promote the library as a "great place to be."[12]

Like a Tweet, the appeal for teen volunteers is brief, its title provides status (i.e., we value your opinion), states a few things that the library advertiser believes that teens like to do (i.e., lead, buy, create, participate, and promote with others). The posting contains multiple neighborhood places to volunteer because TAG operates at five different branches, and it closes with an ability to register electronically during the very first visit to the website.

Librarian Tricia Suellentrop writes the following about teen volunteers in *SLJ*:

> The more experience teens acquire, the more meaningful that experience and the more likely they are to become caring, competent adults. You don't have to begin with a program involving hundreds of teens. Start small—but just start. The enthusiasm and energy of your teen volunteers, even if they're just a handful, will lead you in the right direction.[13]

Hoole Library shows a different technique for motivating college students to become volunteers. The recruitment strategy is technological and entwined in social media. Students can help the library by tagging photos in the library collection. Students access the photos and tagging software from the library's website. The website's moving billboard is presented as a familiar electronic tool, and the recruitment term "crowd sourcing" is a familiar category of electronic participation known to many college students. The library then offers students the opportunity to help test the library website plus the options of free use of library computers and social media links.[14]

RECRUITMENT DEMOGRAPHICS

Along with knowledge of what motivates people to volunteer, recruitment works better if library recruiters know something about the demographic composition of possible volunteers. Dummies.com, in its volunteers' how-to manual, suggests the changes taking place: The classic stereotype of a volunteer is someone who has lots of time to spare and is looking for something to do. Although this perception may have been generally true in the past, when many women stayed out of the workplace and gave their energies to charity, the stereotype no longer fits.[15] Women still volunteer more than men, and people between the ages of 35 and 44 are the likeliest to volunteer. Those members of the "likeliest group" also are likely to be balancing careers with raising of families, not to mention taking care of aging parents, going to the gym, and keeping up with e-mail.

Remember that volunteering is based on both free time and prior experience—both personal and individually witnessed. So volunteering demographics is never simple. For example, better-educated women are more likely to volunteer, but many of these have recently suffered downturns in their family incomes and they have less free time. The population is growing older overall, and older persons volunteer less than younger persons. Minorities, most notably Hispanics, Asians, and African Americans, make up a greater percentage of the population than previously; and these groups volunteer at markedly lower rates than do whites. All of these economic and demographic trends, varying somewhat through the various U.S. regions, suggest that the greater need for volunteers is coming at a time when the sources for volunteers in your locale are changing. One thing is certain: Old volunteer lessons may be out of date, so be careful of whose advice you take.

One more point needs to be included in this discussion of volunteer demographics. To put the issue succinctly, men and women volunteers place value on different aspects of their voluntary experience: A recent study found that:

> Social group inclusion and overall participation in organizational events were the strongest predictors of female volunteers' future intentions to volunteer whereas event participation, being included in the organization's information network, and participating in decision making were the strongest predictors for male volunteers.[16]

WHERE TO RECRUIT

Family Members/Library Users: The first/best answer to "Where to Recruit" is "Close to Home." A good place to find youthful recruits is through families whose members already use your library. Postings at checkout and reference desks, on information bulletin boards, on notices pinned up in meeting rooms—all ought to indicate that you are looking for youth and for older family members as well obtain volunteer recruits. Teri Switzer, dean of the Kraemer Family Library, notes, "Our volunteers are vital links to the UCCS [University of Colorado at Colorado Springs] and Colorado Springs communities and strengthen the programs and services we provide."[17] And, "it is more likely that you will succeed in persuading these persons to volunteer than complete strangers. In sales terms, there is a big difference between a 'cold' call to a stranger than a 'warm' call to an acquaintance or a friend."[18]

Children and Youth: First, young people volunteer more than adults. About 55 percent of those under 18 volunteer, compared to 29 percent of all adults. Second, youth volunteers feel more engaged with their communities than those who do not, and they get less involved in risky behavior. Third, youth are driven by a desire to do good for others. Only 5 percent of young people volunteer because of a school requirement. Fourth, adult role models are significant. A youth who has a parent who volunteers is three times more likely to volunteer on a regular basis than one that does not. And, fifth, many need flexibility in their volunteer hours because of other time commitments for school, work, and home.[19]

Trustee and Advisory Boards: You may not have any say in who is on your governance or advisory board, but some officials ask their library administrators to suggest possible nominees. Being able to provide such a list usually is a great advantage to library administrators. As it does with so many issues, Energize has useful documents and referrals on this subject.[20] Corporate officials with donor contacts, particularly those with legal or economic knowledge, and potential appointees with prior nonprofit board experience all usually make valuable picks, especially if they are library users or supporters.

Older Persons: Senior volunteers, especially those already retired, do not see the world the same way as they did when they were beholden to an employer for a paycheck. Recruitment strategies that seem right for your organization may seem offensive to them. For example, legal checks on seniors may be more than they are willing to put up with. One such case was reported from Levy County Public Library (Florida) in 2006 when the county government instituted drug tests of all volunteers. When word of the tests got around, the public library's volunteer cadre, almost all of whom were seniors, dropped from 55 to 2. One 80-year-old volunteer noted, "It's not like we are a high-risk group for coming in drunk or high or stoned or whatever."[21]

College students: There are some tasks for which we will never have enough staff. One example: What would we need if we really were to be serious about running a reading-centered children's library in a public library or a research centered library in a university library. Who can we actually use except volunteers to staff such ongoing, useful projects? Both of this volume's authors have worked in on-campus volunteer programs; we know that many college kids want to volunteer. Usually such persons—whether fresh out of high school, or older returnees to college—want to get experience in the "real" world. Why shouldn't libraries offer them options to help peers within their study fields or their areas of interest and special training so those people could become more competent in all kinds of ways?

Other Specialized Volunteers: Your library may need other more specialized volunteer categories. If you have a need, define the jobs and recruit them. Use your knowledge of your organization's needs and community assets to help recruit specialized volunteers. And, no matter which categories you want to recruit, don't do dumb recruitment.

- Example: The volunteers are all white, the users involved in volunteer programs are persons of color.
- Example: The volunteers speak English. The users speak Eritrean, Spanish, or Korean.
- Example: Your traditional volunteers want a cloistered (i.e., "silence is golden") library. Your teen users come to the library mainly to work together, which often involves talking and giggling. You surely will have no trouble thinking of others.

Unneeded Volunteer Recruits. When you get volunteer offers that you cannot use, unless you have a training program set up with available openings ready for those after training, tell prospects that you do not have meaningful work for the volunteers at the present time. And, then provide suggestions where the prospects might be able to obtain the work or training opportunities that they are seeking. That can be a regularly updated printed list issued by your volunteer manager, and it can be local, regional, national, and international websites that have volunteer and internship opportunities available. In other words, even when you say no, you build your credibility with those wanting to help you.

Expand the Prospective Volunteer Pool

In nearly every community, you can expand the number of prospective volunteers by redefining who you will accept. Here are some ways to expand your number of prospects.

- Accept recruits from volunteer placement programs.
- Accept community service volunteers from local traffic courts.
- Accept and train employees and volunteers from partnership organizations to do library work.
- Redefine library work—What work is skilled? What work can and should volunteers do?
- Create new worker categories like homework helpers and technology assistants with duties that can be handled by volunteers.
- Redefine library jobs to increase upward mobility.
- Institute flex-time to open up prospects of who can be hired and who can volunteer when.
- Implement virtual work—i.e., work from schools or home.
- Expand time of potential volunteers—e.g., furnish free day care to parents with young children while they volunteer.

Different kinds of recruitment can take on even more general characteristics. Rick Lynch and Steve McCurley suggest that if you want to do "warm body recruitment"—that is, if you need a large number of relatively unskilled volunteers—you might use brochures, posters, or recruit groups. If you need volunteers with special skills or demographic characteristics, such as community economic influentials, known donors, and civic leaders, you need to ask individuals personally and plan your recruitment more carefully. This also includes volunteers who represent ethnic, linguistic, or racial diversity.[22]

ONLINE VOLUNTEER RECRUITMENT

In her book, *Best of All: The Quick Reference Guide to Effective Volunteer Involvement*, Linda Graff writes:

> Technology provides organizations with new ways to reach out to new populations of volunteers; it offers a myriad of ways to connect with, and provide support to, existing volunteers; it raises expectations regarding response time and deadlines; it is *the* method of communication for some, often younger, population segments; it is a must-use element for the volunteer leader.[23]

The Internet is increasingly important in volunteer recruitment. Here are a couple of realities:

> the Internet is playing a major role in matching up potential **volunteers** with the organizations that most need help. One of the largest sites, idealist.org, boasts a half million members who support some 84,000 nonprofits in more than 180 countries[24]

In designing your website recruiting tool, make sure that you have sufficient access points so that even casual visitors will be directed to content sites.

In volunteer recruitment on the web, assume that visitors may just be browsing, so the need is to arrest their attention from the moment they arrive. On many websites, more than 50 percent of the traffic comes directly into a page other than the home page.

Traditional hierarchical relations, therefore, may not be appropriate on your volunteer's page. You need to assume that new recruits will arrive at many different points; you need to guide them to vital information about your website. The most important indicator in regarding the accessibility of an up-to-date library website is to ask how its designers have allowed or encouraged access to it. There are publications that can help you assess this issue.[25]

To sum up, an outstanding library website is marketed through blogs, wikis, and electronic postings of every kind, in an attempt to capture users in need and encourage them to become current or remain continuing library website customers. The second feature of this multiplicity of tags sent into the electronic world is that they are connected to the specific information needed or wanted; they do not force persons to enter through the library's introductory web page. And the sites continue that multiplicity of linking within the website, allowing people to move about to find exactly what they want and need. In other words, the library website should make it obvious and easy to sign up to be a library volunteer.

ONLINE VOLUNTEER SITES

Online volunteer recruitment is a big business, one in which libraries ought to be more involved than they are. The box below contains a list of online sites where libraries can (and do) post their volunteer job description needs. These include sites with the titles of *Idealist*, *Network for Good*, *Volunteer Solutions*, *Volunteers of America*, *Volunteer Match*, and *Points of Light*. Library professionals can be assured of some future developments. Libraries are going to be more online, collaborative, and international in the future. In support of this generalization, consider the following volunteer websites. These represent the kind of national/international view of volunteerism that libraries will likely have to adopt in the years ahead.

Serve.gov (http://serve.gov): This is the national initiative, "United We Serve," designed "to help meet growing social needs resulting from the economic downturn." Libraries can create projects and recruit volunteers.

All for Good (http://www.allforgood.org): All for Good is created by web designers, and it provides an open platform for finding volunteer opportunities. The apps allow the users to narrow volunteer opportunities by when you can volunteer.

Idealist.org (http://www.idealist.org): Idealist.org is a project of Action Without Borders. In addition to searching for opportunities or posting your library's needs, you can start a volunteer affinity group.

Seattle.gov (http://www.seattle.gov): Your city, county, or state may have a volunteer portal. For example, Seattle.gov offers a list of volunteer opportunities. Volunteers find opportunities to help at the aquarium and with recycling, general cleanups, the courts, the pea patch gardens, parks, the public library, urban creeks, the zoo, or with tutoring.

Youth Service America (http://servenet.org) Founded in 1996 to help facilitate volunteering by young people in 155 countries, this resource is in its fifth iteration. It now connects users via blogs, newsfeeds, and mobile messaging. As youthful as you can be, check out the iBelong page, where those interested build personal customizable pages for their volunteer profiles. Step aside, Facebook, while we enter the world of deeply meaningful social media.[26]

Large cities—and increasingly smaller communities as well—also have a way to match volunteers with organizations looking for them. Baltimore, Maryland, for example, has Volunteer Central. The United Way is always a good place to start to see if that agency maintains a volunteer recruitment site. For example, the United Way of King County, the location of Seattle, bears the cross-top banner, "We bring caring people together to give, volunteer, and take action to help people in need and solve our community's toughest challenges."[27]

Some libraries may already be using these sites to advertise for library volunteers or recruit individuals who post on these sites to become volunteers at the library. These sites seem likely to be good at locating well-educated, tech-competent college students and twentysomethings. Graff is right; this is our future, so we should get e-fluent when we recruit volunteers, or get a group of volunteers to explore using and managing these sites.

Your library should always have an online volunteer presence. The Alameda County (California) Library takes only one page to recruit potential volunteers, part of a solid online overall representation of the library, its operations, and opportunities. The page highlights the volunteer jobs available (Senior Services, Bootleggers for K–8 classes, Internet docents who help users with the web, and Kid Power programs that are part of the summer reading program.)[28]

This online recruitment announcement is typical for libraries. Obviously, it brings success because it has been "up" for quite a long time in the world of electronic communication. Whether you are a large or small library, this kind of electronic announcement suggests the need for your staff who answer phones to know about the advertisement's claims and the programs they represent. They particularly need to know how these claims play out in the neighborhoods and organizational configurations of individual branches. Without such staff training, potential volunteers who haven't gotten the information they need will tell others that the library electronic poster is just a "put-off" if there is no infrastructure to handle their inquiry.

RECRUITMENT WITH AND FROM PARTNERS

If all the library stars are in the right order, a well-developed and well-run volunteer program can do numerous things in partnership that it cannot do alone. One notable example occurred in 2009, when California public libraries, organized by the California State Library (CSL), teamed up with California VolunteerMatch.[29]

The CSL-VolunteerMatch partnership was on the right track. The partnership (1) promoted libraries as hubs for civic engagement, (2) strengthened their capacity to utilize skilled volunteers through training, and (3) raised awareness of Californians about library volunteer opportunities by advertising library volunteer options on the California VolunteerMatch website, which then was getting 10 million hits annually. The partnership resulted in the establishment of a new joint website, http://www.volunteermatch.org, that makes it easier for Californians to volunteer at local libraries and at other nonprofits within the libraries communities. The partnership started right with a two-day training seminar on volunteer engagement for California library administrators. CSL public information officer Laura Parker noted, "Volunteer engagement benefits both the library and the community. In their role as information center and community living room, libraries are well positioned to serve as hubs for civic engagement. . . . We believe this is a program that other states will want to learn from and implement."[30]

The partnership was marked by an increase in electronic recruitment. The new publicity promoted public libraries as civic hubs. By positioning libraries as such hubs, the program promoted skilled volunteering in public libraries and strengthened the capacity of libraries to utilize skilled volunteers. The joint website allowed library outlets to advertise their volunteer openings to more than 10 million visitors in the VolunteerMatch network. And, libraries in turn promoted http://california libraries.volunteermatch.org to library patrons as a resource for finding volunteer opportunities with 65,000 participating organizations.

One special appeal of the California partnership was to baby boomers who were looking for what has been termed "proactive volunteerism." "Engagement means a set of services," says Amy Ryan, director of the Hennepin County Library (HCL) in suburban Minneapolis, which launched a program for seniors called 55+. "It's about programs, yes, but it's also about volunteerism and partnerships with other organizations. What libraries can provide and expect back from older patrons is likely more than they've imagined, especially when it comes to boomers."[31]

WHO NOT TO RECRUIT

A few decades ago, Barbara O'Neill, an extension professor at Rutgers, wrote an article about volunteers to avoid. Here is who she recommends against recruiting:

- *The Know-it-All.* While they're really amateurs when dealing with a particular topic, know-it-alls view themselves as perfectly competent.
- *The Name-Dropper*: This type of volunteer, too, is motivated entirely by self-interest. Name-droppers like to "collect" affiliations they can use in self-promoting.
- *The Complainer*: People who constantly complain . . . Sooner or later, they'll start complaining about you.[32]

To O'Neill's three, we add another group, the Hidden Bosses. These are volunteers who believe that the library staff should perform as their paid servants. Often referring to their close associations with an administrator or governance official or their relationships with the volunteer coordinator who usually is close to the system's administration, they tell staff what to do or how to do it in matters related to their projects, sometimes even extending to personal services such as rides to and from their volunteer position, getting takeout food orders, and carrying messages.

Here are a few recruitment tips that can head off some volunteer-related problems before they occur:

- Recruit volunteers with forethought. Decide on the tasks that they need to do and write a job description for each position. When recruiting volunteers by mail, send them a job description with your letter of invitation. Or, point out that the job description is posted on your library's website.
- Promote volunteer opportunities that last for brief periods of time. Start with a short assignment that can be ended or extended by mutual agreement.
- Never feel so "desperate" for volunteers that you neglect to fully orient them on their assignment.
- Ask "cold-callers" who volunteer to teach a class or send a proposal describing their ideas in writing. This will quickly separate the name-droppers and the "hot ideas" crowds from serious volunteers.

APPLICATION CONTENT

Allen County (Fort Wayne, Indiana) has a brief, succinct volunteer application on its website that is well worth examining as a model. All you have to do is look at a brief description of the volunteer program and be over the age of 13, and you can apply online. (See http://www.acpl.lib.in.us/volunteer/index.html.)

This clever volunteer application page, reprintable as a counter piece or mailer, sets the tone for the program and the library: Our volunteers help staff to deliver quality service to patrons. The heaviest limitation (age 13) is stated as a subordinate clause, and the age 18 permission statement is put off until such time as a student-age person is accepted for volunteer work. Finally, the message sheet closes with an affirmation of personal benefits that volunteers receive when they work with the library. And, all of this takes only 257 words.

We have summarized a few other electronic applications worth examining, comparing them to that of Allen County.

Compare this volunteer work solicitation with the application from the University of Memphis Library, which asks for one's Social Security number not once, but twice. The application includes a statement about conditions that might cause the library to sue the volunteer. No doubt the library is forced to use this unseemly application by the university's legal position as a state school. That reality, alas, does not make the tone of the library application less formidable, especially when the library is competing with dozens of other not-for-profit agencies that use less onerous language in their volunteer applications.[33]

Fairfax County (Virginia) Public Library tries to get every possible information need met in a single form, the "Volunteer Application." Depending on how you count the words and the sizes of the empty boxes that need to be filled, this form is somewhere between two and four pages long. There are spaces for all address information, including e-mail addresses; a listing of education, both K–12 and university degrees; a "Skills" section, with boxes for computers, foreign languages, and "Other" skills; and another page of questions and boxes after that. In short, this volunteer application reads like a fairly substantial employment application, and the friendliest note in the application form is the end line, which reads: "The library will use the personal information you provide solely to assist us in finding the best volunteer placement for you."[34]

Hennepin County is one of any number of libraries that uses a listing of categorical openings for volunteers as a way to give possible applicants some notion about the activities in which they might have the opportunity to engage. Like Fairfax County public libraries, Hennepin County uses the "long" application form to gather information on a potential volunteer. Hennepin also has a section asking the applicant to declare her or his criminal history.

The intriguing section of the Hennepin County volunteer application, however, is the 500+-word section entitled "Your Rights as a Subject of Data." This section, it is declared, is included because, "In accordance with the Minnesota Government Data Practices Act, we are informing you of your rights as a subject of data. The data you give us about yourself is needed to identify you and assist in determining your suitability for the volunteer position(s) for which you are applying."[35] Putting this section of the form into perspective, doesn't it really say the following? "Oh, yes, and by the way, if you think we have discriminated against you and want to sue the library, here is what you should show your attorney to get started." And, "Oh, yes, we'd love to have you as a volunteer for Hennepin County Library."

In this array of volunteer applications, you can see how different public libraries in different states and within different communities operate in ways so completely separate that they mirror complete differences in operating philosophies. American humorist and author Mark Twain (1835–1910) allegedly said, "The difference between the right word and the almost right word is the difference between lightning and a lightning bug."[36] So too are the "little differences" that demonstrate the vast separation between U.S. libraries in the way they approach and acclimate volunteers into their important work. When one searches for lightning in library volunteer literature, we too often find lightning bugs where we need far more illumination and clarity.

Though many school libraries let students sign up to volunteer with no application, it is a good idea to get a parent's approval and get a little information from a teacher who knows the student. Most schools require adults working in the library to agree to a criminal background check and stress the need to commit to regular hours for at least a semester.

VOLUNTEER TURNOVER AND RETENTION

Once recruited, it is important that volunteers be retained and that the library reduces volunteer turnover. Libraries will always see volunteers leaving their programs for personal reasons—change in job, family, or moving away from the library's neighborhood. But libraries should minimize the number of people who leave the volunteer program because they are bored or don't like the experience. There are several things that should be done to keep volunteers in the library.

"Right"-Sizing the Commitments of Volunteers

In 2002, Susan Ellis and Steve McCurley pointed out that volunteering had moved from "Long Term" periods to "Short Term" periods in a process that occurred between 1975 and 1998. That change modified the amount of effort and skill needed to manage a volunteer program. The two authors write, "The Short Term Volunteer who typically serves for shorter periods has been accompanied by an increased need for good volunteer management, with greater demands on the agency for accommodating the needs of the newer type of volunteers. This trend has dominated volunteer management during the past decade and will continue to influence volunteer programs for the foreseeable future."[37]

Libraries need to understand what type of commitment their volunteers prefer to make. If volunteers aren't able to commit to months of volunteering, it makes more sense to organize volunteer jobs into shorter units. While it might be easier for libraries to create volunteer jobs that last for a semester, for the school year, or for the whole summer, this might not be how volunteers view their commitment. The challenge is to allow for varying time commitments while still getting the work done. Talk to volunteers or potential volunteers about what is the "right" commitment and plan accordingly.

Special Emphasis on Communication

It is imperative to add communication to the volunteer program planning equation because, more than with many other library programs, the success of the volunteer program depends on good institutional communication with volunteers. Volunteer retention, especially at the beginning of the program or its major changes, depends on successful communication with potential or new volunteers. As mentioned in Chapter 4, staff need to be trained to communicate with volunteers every time they work at the library. The library may also publish a volunteer newsletter (perhaps this task could be assigned to a volunteer), have regular volunteer meetings at which volunteers find out about new library programs and services, or have a way for volunteers to ask questions. You can also communicate electronically for volunteers who have e-mail or use Facebook or Twitter. Each volunteer should choose the best avenue for communication with the library.

In addition to general information of library updates, the library should have a way to communicate with volunteers for emergencies or changes in schedule. Nothing is more of a turnoff than for a volunteer to make the effort to show up for work at the library only to find that the library is unexpectedly closed, the supervisor is ill, or the schedule has been changed. For each volunteer, there should be a staff member who knows how to reach them to let them know about changes.

Set volunteer work into the regular reporting scheme of the library to count volunteer hours, note startup and completion of volunteer project tasks, and report on any problems or issues that need to be made part of management consciousness regarding volunteers. Keeping the volunteer program organized helps volunteers understand what they are supposed to do and to feel as if what they accomplish is valued. Have a clear and guilt-free way for volunteers to ask questions or complain.

And the twin to this is to make sure that there is follow-through so questions get answered and complaints acknowledged.

The assumption of this program is that the better the volunteer experience is, the more people who experience it will want to continue to be part of it. There is, of course, an additional way to enhance the volunteer experience—to expand the benefits of the experience. Here are a few examples, both general and specific to a couple of programs.

- *Access to staff perks*: Parking, lounge, restroom, lunchroom. More access to staff in relative leisure helps volunteers learn more about the library's operations.
- *Staff checkout rights*: Volunteers treated like staff in materials circulation.
- *Meet with director and supervisors in social settings*: Get "insider information." For many volunteers, a meeting with the manager of the library is as important as meeting the mayor or the school superintendent. Lunch and a tour with the director or upper-level administrators are usually very attractive to volunteers.
- *Collegiality*: Treated in the library with the respect of another library worker.
- *Awards*: An award offers concrete evidence for your appreciation of volunteer contributions (see below).

If you operate a successful, high-visibility program, turnover should be minimal and retention should be easy. One route to success is the operation of a high-visibility program that in the normal course of its operations—because of your publicity releases about its activities or the word-of-mouth publicity that your volunteers give to their relatives and friends—you transform your volunteer program into a "buyers' market." In other words, more potential new volunteers appear than you want or need. Recruitment becomes a matter of simply contacting persons who already have demonstrated their interest in volunteering for your organization by filling out a form or some other act of self-identification.

The final word on volunteer retention goes to the United Parcel Service Foundation, which did a simple survey about retention in 1998. The survey found that the principal reason that persons gave for leaving was "conflicts with more pressing demands," but all the reasons for leaving boiled down to organizational ineptitude.[38] The list included:

Charity was not well managed:	26 percent
Charity did not use volunteer's time well:	23 percent
Charity did not use volunteer's talents well:	18 percent
Volunteer tasks were not clearly defined:	16 percent
Volunteers were not thanked:	9 percent[39]

To sum up, poor volunteer management practices result in more lost volunteers than people losing interest because of changing personal and family needs. The best way for volunteer organizations to receive more hours of volunteer services is to be careful managers of the time already being volunteered by people of all ages and from all strata of our volunteer society.

VOLUNTEER RECOGNITION

Some volunteers don't need or expect recognition, but libraries should find ways to thank and honor *all* volunteers. Many libraries also have ways to acknowledge extraordinary volunteer efforts. Recognition can be simple or elaborate, but it needs to be planned and executed at least annually.

The simplest recognition, of course, is to say thank you every time someone volunteers. Supervising staff should be trained to do this and encouraged to be specific about something the volunteer has done. For example, a staff person might say "Thank you for stamping all these books, it means that the new books can go on the shelf today!" This is Etiquette 101, but it makes a difference. Another simple form of recognition is to give a certificate to each volunteer confirming the number of hours worked and recognizing their efforts.

Some libraries hold events to thank volunteers. The Seminole Community College (St. Petersburg, Florida) library invites volunteers to "an annual Volunteer Appreciation Luncheon to publicly recognize and thank volunteers for their valuable service. A catered meal, gifts, public recognition, and enjoyable entertainment are featured at each luncheon as an expression of genuine gratitude for all that our volunteers do for the Library."[40]

Some libraries give volunteer awards and/or nominate library volunteers for community, university, or school district awards. Washoe County School District (Reno, Nevada) gives out an Exceptional Volunteer Award to several people or groups each year. Volunteers must serve a minimum of 100 hours and not receive educational credit for volunteering. Nominations are made by staff who describe the volunteer's contributions and link the volunteer to school improvement. Awards are presented monthly at a district Board of Trustees meeting. Award recipients receive an award proclamation, board pin, and thank you gifts as available.[41]

Or, libraries can recognize all volunteers by noting the number of hours they have donated. Jefferson County Public Library (Missouri) makes this kind of award. The library recognizes volunteers twice a year. Volunteers who complete 100 hours get a certificate. For 200 hours, the volunteer receives a certificate and a bookplate for a new book in the library's collection. There are varying awards for other hour amounts and, at 1,000 hours, a letter of appreciation, a bookplate, a news release, an individual plaque, and inclusion of name on a plaque in the library honoring those who have volunteered for 1,000 hours.[42]

Libraries may have a combination of ways to thank and recognize volunteers. Teens may get a pizza party at the end of the summer, organizations might get a letter of thanks (or a board proclamation) documenting the hours and the impact of its donation, and seniors might get reserved seating at popular library events. Whatever your library does, be consistent, thank everyone, and find fun ways to celebrate your volunteers. And, of course, publicize what you do to recognize volunteers both within the library and externally—it will make it easier to recruit and retain volunteers in the future.

Recruitment, retention, and recognition are the cornerstones of any successful volunteer program. Smaller libraries will be able to be less formal than larger programs in the policies and procedures they create for operating the volunteer program. Every library should have a plan for recruitment, retention, and recognition that staff can use to maximize volunteer satisfaction and increase the impact of the volunteers' efforts on behalf of the library.

NOTES

1. "Thus Said in Chicago: Mayor Daley Champions Libraries," *American Libraries*, June 2006, 27.

2. The background for this section is from World Volunteer Web, "Benefits of Volunteering," http://www.worldvolunteerweb.org/resources/how-to-guides/volunteer/doc/benefits-of-volunteering.html (accessed April 27, 2012).

3. Katerina Papadakis, Tonya Griffin, and Joel Frater, "Understanding Volunteers' Motivations," *Proceedings of the 2004 Northeastern Recreation Research Symposium*, http://www.fs.fed.us/ne/newtown_square/publications/technical_reports/pdfs/2005/326papers/papadakis326.pdf (accessed March 17, 2013).

4. Volunteer Match, "20 Reasons to Volunteer," http://www.volunteermatch.org/volunteers/resources/tipstricks.jsp (accessed May 10, 2013).

5. Richard B. Freeman, "Working for Nothing: The Supply of Volunteer Labor," NBER Working Paper No. 5435 (Washington, DC: National Bureau of Economic Research, Issued January 1996). Published in *Journal of Law and Education* 15, no. 1, pt. 2 (January 1997): S140–S166.

6. Deng Yan (Library of Hunan Institute of Science and Technology, Yueyang 414006, China), "On the Development of Volunteer Spirit of Library," *Library Work and Study*, April 2008, http://en.cnki.com.cn/Article_en/CJFDTOTAL-TSGG200804003.htm (accessed December 24, 2009). This paper carries this motivating idea, as exemplified in preparation to host the 2008 Olympics, as a way to examine library volunteerism.

7. Nicholas D. Kristoff, "Our Basic Human Pleasures: Food, Sex and Giving," *New York Times*, January 17, 2010, http://www.nytimes.com/2010/01/17/opinion/17kristof.html?th&emc=th (accessed January 18, 2010).

8. "Volunteering to Help Others Could Lead to Better Health," APA Press Release, September 6, 2011, http://www.apa.org/news/press/releases/2011/09/volunteering-health.aspx (accessed March 15, 2013).

9. Chris Jarvis, "Want Good Volunteers? Forget the Altruistic, Find the Self-Interested" (Part 1 of 2). *Realized Worth*, December 2, 2009, http://www.realizedworth.com/2009/09/want-good-volunteers-forget-altruistic.html (accessed January 20, 2013).

10. Volunteer Match, "Be a Great Volunteer," http://www.volunteermatch.org/volunteers/resources/tipstricks.jsp (accessed October 27, 2012).

11. Corporation for National and Community Service (CNCS), 2009, http://www.nationalservice.gov/.

12. Vancouver Public Library, Teen Advisory Group page, http://www.vpl.ca/events/details/teen_advisory_group (accessed March 17, 2013).

13. Tricia Suellentrop, "Step Right Up: A Volunteer Program Can Add Value to a Teen's Life," *School Library Journal*, December 1, 2007, http://www.schoollibraryjournal.com/article/CA6505672.htm (accessed July 4, 2011).

14. University of Alabama, Hoole Library, http://www.lib.ua.edu/libraries/hoole/ (accessed March 17, 2013).

15. Dummies.com, "Making Everything Easier: Considering Why People Volunteer," http://www.dummies.com/how-to/content/considering-why-people-volunteer.html (accessed October 27, 2012.

16. Richard D. Waters and Denise Sevick Bortree, "Improving Volunteer Retention Efforts in Public Library Systems: How Communication and Inclusion Impact Female and Male Volunteers Differently," *International Journal of Nonprofit and Voluntary Sector Marketing* 17, no. 2, (May 2012): 92–107.

17. University of Colorado at Colorado Springs, Kraemer Family Library, "Volunteer in the Library," http://www.uccs.edu/library/info/volunteer.html (accessed March 23, 2013).

18. Joanne Fritz, "Recruiting Volunteers—Three Approaches," http://nonprofit.about.com/od/volunteers/a/recruitvols.htm (accessed August 3, 2013).

19. Joanne Fritz, "Top Six Facts about Youth Volunteers," About.com Nonprofit Charity Organizations, http://nonprofit.about.com/od/volunteers/tp/youthvol.htm (accessed March 23, 2013).

20. Energize, "Boards of Directors and Working with Committees," http://www.energizeinc.com/art/subj/boards.html (accessed May 12, 2013).

21. Norman Oder, "Drug Test Policy Deters Volunteers," *Library Journal*, 131, no. 18 (November 1, 2006): 15.

22. Rick Lynch and Steve McCurley, *Essential Volunteer Management* (Downers Grove, IL: Heritage Arts Press, 1998).

23. Linda L. Graff, *Best of All: The Quick Reference Guide to Effective Volunteer Involvement* (Hamilton, Ontario: Linda L. Graff & Associates, 2005). The book is available both on paper and electronically.

24. Alex Kingsbury, "Find Your Volunteer Niche," *U.S. News and World Report* 147, no. 11 (December 2010).

25. Jeff Lash, "How Did You Get Here?" *Web Design Magazine*, June 4, 2003, http://www.digital-web.com/articles/how_did_you_get_here/ (accessed October 11, 2009).

26. Cecilia Hogan, "For Our Next (Charitable) Trick, We'll Need a Volunteer," http://www.infotoday.com/searcher/jun10/Hogan.shtml (accessed August 3, 2013).

27. United Way of King County website, http://www.uwkc.org/ (accessed May 13, 2013).

28. Alameda County (CA), "Volunteer Opportunities," http://guides.aclibrary.org/content.php?mode=preview&pid=124482&sid=1147036 (accessed July 2, 2011).

29. "California State Library and VolunteerMatch Team Up to Boost Civic Engagement in Public Libraries," http://www.volunteermatch.org/pressroom?id=516 (accessed May 30, 2010). Also, see *Get Involved: Powered by Your Library*, retrieved from http://www.californialibraries.volunteermatch.org. Some of the activities of CSL in this section were drawn from the California State Library at http://www.library.ca.gov/. Also, see "Library Plugs into Volunteer Power," *St. Helena Star*, http://www.sthelenastar.com/articles/2009/04/23/features/community/doc49e fa6600fb4d744297134.prt. VolunteerMatch also has a separate website at http://www.volunteermatch.org.

30. Ibid.

31. Beth Dempsey, "What Boomers Want," *Library Journal* 132, no. 12 (July 2007): 36–39.

32. Barbara M. O'Neill, "How to Avoid 'Firing' Your Volunteers," *Journal of Extension* 28, no. 3 (Fall 1990), http://www.joe.org/joe/1990fall/a12.php (accessed June 27, 2008).

33. University of Memphis Library website, http://www.memphis.edu/libsupport/volunteers.php (accessed May 14, 2013).

34. https://www.fairfaxcounty.gov/library/volunteer/vol_app.htm (accessed April 30, 2012).

35. https://www.volgistics.com/ex/portal.dll/ap?AP=1837199284 (accessed July 7, 2013).

36. http://www.quotationspage.com/quote/1119.html (accessed April 30, 2013).

37. Susan J. Ellis and Steve McCurley, "Mandated Service—the Future of Volunteering?" *e-Volunteerism: The Journal to Inform and Challenge Leaders of Volunteers* 2, no. 4 (July 2002), http://www.e-volunteerism.com/quarterly/02sum/mandate2c (accessed March 26, 2013).

38. Cited in Steve McCurley and Rick Lynch, *Keeping Volunteers: A Guide to Retention* (London: Directory of Social Change, 2007), 4.

39. Ibid.

40. Seminole Community College website, http://www.spcollege.edu/scl/volunteers.htm (accessed May 15, 2013).

41. Washoe County School District website, http://www.washoe.k12.nv.us/district/departments/volunteering/recognition/awards (accessed May 15, 2013).

42. Jefferson County Public Library website, http://www.jeffersoncountylibrary.org/about-jcl/policies-a-guidelines/147-volunteer_recognition (accessed April 15, 2013).

6

Evaluating Your Volunteer Program

How will you know if your volunteers are successful? You will know because of the same evidence staff and users will see: Your volunteers have brought about improvements. Volunteers have changed the library for the better. A nice summary of this kind of conclusion can be found in the work of the Prosci Change Management organization in an introduction to one of their many seminars. The posting notes, "Change is about moving the organization from a current state to a future state. ... Organizations change ... to achieve results by reaching a future state where performance is better than in the current state. But ... it is only when employees impacted by the change embrace, adopt and use the solution that benefits are realized and value is created."[1]

CALCULATING THE COSTS AND BENEFITS OF VOLUNTEERS

In addition to this practical assessment of your volunteer program, it is important to understand the costs and benefits of your program. Anna Mills, whose questions form the first part of Chapter 4, offers clear guidance on costs. Volunteers always have costs.[2] The first part of that cost is for externalities—recruiting and screening. The second part is internal, i.e., for training and management.

According to a report in *Public/Private Ventures*, the annual cost for a nonprofit to screen, train and manage one volunteer per year is $300.[3] Since most nonprofits— 94 percent—have an annual budget of under $1 million, volunteer management usually takes a back seat to "core functions," and the result is that those willing to serve have fewer valuable opportunities and basic services go undelivered. Such situations often mean trouble in the organization.

Complicating this issue, most libraries chronically underspend on training of all kinds. In private-sector information fields, like real estate and finance, the recommended institutional training budget is generally 5 percent of the institutional gross salary line. Few libraries spend even half that on staff training.[4] Coming at this issue from the TQM (Total Quality Management) approach for libraries, Despina Wilson suggests that 3 percent of the total salary line is the minimum of cost for training library staff.[5] Training for volunteers should be about the same percentage of the volunteer budget.

Costs of Volunteer Supervision—Some Ratios

If you just "dump" volunteers into your organization, expecting staff at the work sites to train them for volunteer tasks by simple mentoring and to "supervise" them along with all the other work tasks that they perform, you will end up with huge variations in the quality of various pieces of your volunteer program. Appropriate supervision of volunteers is critical to the successful operation of a program, and balancing the ratio of staff to volunteers is vital to that supervision.

Here are some examples of the ratio (i.e., the limits) of supervisor to volunteers:

- Court Appointed Special Advocates for Children (CASA) says "that you need to have an adequate staff to volunteer ratio to ensure timely and thorough case management. The ratio specified in the National CASA Program Standards is one supervisor to 30 volunteers."[6]
- Catholic Relief Services (CRS) has a lower ratio: "In the experience of CRS staff, a common supervisor to volunteer ratio is 1:10."[7]
- Cheyenne Mountain Zoo has a still lower ratio. "The ratio of adult supervisors to youth should be 1 to 5, depending on the age of the group's participants—so they are under constant supervision."[8] Supervising volunteers can be a safety issue. As we were finishing this book, a volunteer caretaker in a wild animal rescue haven in California lost her life when a lion attacked her. She was not supervised.[9] Library work is usually not inherently dangerous, but young people especially need conscientious supervision to ensure their safety.
- Charlotte Mecklenburg Library's Matthews Library currently has 12 full-time equivalent staff and a volunteer team of 81 volunteers that donated six hours of volunteer service time in October 2010 (6.8 volunteers to 1 staff member ratio). At the Davidson Branch, a "ratio of 12 volunteers for every 1 staff member is the highest such ratio system-wide and is notable because of the relative size of the staff and square footage of this facility."[10]

So what ratio is optimal for your library? At the very least, volunteers need to have an institutional sense of where they fit into the organization's service and support work. There also is the need to orient volunteer newcomers to the legal regulations for health and safety with which the library complies. Next, they need training on how to speak on behalf of the organization. Finally, they need training on how to work successfully within your library's organizational style.

The costs of this training are not inconsequential, and training costs ought not to be minimized. Training is one of the primary reasons why many persons volunteer. There also are communication costs—whether by electronic means or by bulk mailings—and record keeping. Similarly volunteer programs have "overhead charges" for office supplies, space (office, meeting, storage and parking), insurance and other "hidden" costs. Lastly, most successful volunteer programs spend money

Table 6.1

Examples of Volunteer Costing—Costs Are Illustrative

Item	Adult Volunteer (Cost per volunteer per year)	Student Volunteers (Cost per volunteer per year)	Groups* (Cost per group)	Interns (Cost per intern per semester)
Recruitment: Flyers, reception, newspaper ad, class visits, security check, staff time	$50	$25	$25	$25
Training: Name tag, volunteer handbook, staff time	$100	$75	$10	$75
Supervision: staff time—15 minutes per session/hour/week, troubleshooting as needed	$200 ($5 × 40 sessions)	$250 ($5 × 50 hours)	$20 ($5 × 4 hours)	$60 ($5 per week for 12 weeks)
Volunteer/Staff Recognition	$10	$10	$3	$10
Total	$360 for 120 hours	$360 for 50 hours	$48 for 4 hours × # in group	$170 for a 12-week project

*Groups include United Way work groups, service groups, professional groups, church groups. These are usually one-time-only or project-oriented sessions.

to thank volunteers for their service, recognition that includes costs of food and gifts.

Each library needs to estimate the costs of maintaining its volunteer program and to be aware that each type of volunteer may have a different associated cost. Table 6.1 provides simple examples of the categories of expense that need to be included in the cost of volunteer programs.

Mark Hager and Jeffrey Brudney in their study (cited previously in Chapter 4) find that the expenses of good training and good supervision bring positive results. They write, "Organizations that … adopted more volunteer management practices had higher net benefits than organizations that had adopted fewer. Organizations with an identifiable coordinator had higher net benefits than organizations without such a coordinator. Both findings point to the value of investing in volunteer management capacity."[11]

Through the past decade and a half, there has been a growing trend to calculate dollar measurements to the costs and benefits of library services and products. The authors of this volume played an active role in this effort for many years, eventually producing an ALA book on the subject.[12] This continuing effort is important, especially since it yields a high-visibility, easily understood expression of the public value of libraries.

Table 6.2

Charlotte Mecklenburg Library Benefits from Volunteer Services

	Number of Individual Volunteers	Hours Donated	Value of Hours	Notes	% Increase Hours Donated over Previous Year
FY07	708	15,460.71	$271,491.56	Value based on $17.55/hr.	
FY08	681	14,219.51	$247,356.42	Value based on $17.55/hr.	-8%
FY09	988	25,047.87	$431,476.15	Value based on $17.55/hr.	76%
FY10	957	27,019.10	$547,136.78	Value based on $20.25/hr.	8%
FY11 Goal	1500	54,038.20	$1,094,273.55	Value based on $20.25/hr.	**Projected 100%**

Note: Overall, a 75% increase in volunteer hours contributed, FY07–FY10. Equivalent in hours to 13 full-time equivalent staff in FY10.

Source: Karen Beach, "Volunteer Utilization Report Prepared for Future of the Library Task Force of the Charlotte Mecklenburg Library, 2010," *Public Library Quarterly* 32, no. 2 (2013): 150–62, http://www.tandfonline.com/doi/abs/10.1080/01616846.2013.788960?af=R#.Uid9pNJzG9F (accessed September 4, 2013).

Library volunteer services need this mathematical attention. One way to speak about the results of volunteerism is through calculation of the net benefits of a program. A net benefit is the difference between the benefits that volunteers bring to charities and the costs of recruitment and management of volunteers for the organization. "Net benefits are easy to calculate. As an evaluation tool, it lends itself to comparison and benchmarking across a variety of volunteer programs and sponsoring nonprofit organizations."[13] One limiting caveat: "While individual volunteer duties defy direct comparison across different organizations, common elements in volunteer administration and the benefits that volunteers bring to nonprofits lend themselves to measurement and comparison."[14]

One effective report of value added by library volunteers is found in a 2010 report from the Charlotte Mecklenburg (North Carolina) Library (CML). In this report, CML staff examined the specific value added to public library services by the work of their volunteer cadre. That study has been reported to the citizens of Charlotte Mecklenburg[15] and to the readers of an academic journal as well.[16] Table 6.2 was taken from that study.

Charlotte Mecklenburg Library does an outstanding job of conveying the economic benefits of volunteers to the library organization in this brief form, which is based on simple arithmetic calculations. Rather than make its own estimates of the value of volunteer time, CML uses a valuation from a national organization that makes such calculations for all states.[17] It is easy to see the annual performance of volunteers and the expectations of benefits built into the thinking of CML leaders. To calculate net benefits, Charlotte Mecklenburg would subtract the costs of the volunteer program from the assigned dollar value of the contributions their volunteers make.

LIBRARY OUTCOME PLANNING AND EVALUATION

Once you conceptualize volunteer programs, deal with the practical concerns about costs in your library, and have estimated costs, you are ready to write a draft volunteer outcome plan. This process involves setting goals, identifying how to evaluate these goals, and setting up an annual review to ensure that the volunteer program is succeeding. Larger libraries, universities, and school districts often have an evaluation method and schedule. In such cases, the volunteer program would be expected to be part of the larger planning and evaluation program. Librarians in smaller libraries may need to create their own plan that suits the volunteer program and their work style.

Start by asking what your goals are for your volunteer program. To set these goals, list what the library hopes to gain and how this supports the library's mission. Make a list of volunteer jobs based on an assessment of the library's needs, what skill level volunteers will need, who on staff has the time and skill to supervise volunteers, and what legal or procedural issues might need to be resolved before volunteers can donate time to the library. In small libraries, this may be as simple as identifying a couple of goals and writing them down to share with the library supervisors. In a larger library, a more formal approach may be called for; and it is wise to involve any staff who will work with volunteers in setting goals.

The next step in planning for your volunteer program is to figure out how you will know if you volunteer program has met its goals. Or, put another way, how will you know your volunteer program is successful—that you have the right volunteers doing the right jobs, and that these jobs make your library better and help you better serve your community?

In outcome planning for each goal, identify an indicator of success. The indicator can be the number of people helped by volunteers, the number of circulations done by volunteers, or how many freshman give high marks to the volunteer-led tour of the library.

Next, figure out what information you need to collect from volunteers (number of hours, tasks completed, number of user contacts, etc.), staff, and users. Decide how often you need to collect this data and how often you need to compile it. For new volunteers or for jobs new to volunteers, you may want to check the data often to be sure progress is being made and that jobs are being done correctly. For seasoned volunteers doing jobs that are "regular" volunteer jobs, you might only need to check the indicators once a year.

Lastly, it is important to gather all the indicator information together and see what is or is not working well. If you have volunteer-led tours, but students can't remember anything they learned or said they did not like the tour, you should figure out how to use this information to make the tours more effective, or stop offering the tours if they can't be improved.

Table 6.3

Outcome Planning for Library Volunteer Programs

Model Elements and Structure		
	Definitions	**Examples**
Outcome	Intended impact	Volunteers will successfully help students find library materials by using the library catalog
Indicator	Observable and measurable behaviors and condition	The number and percentage of students that will successfully use the library catalog with the help of library volunteers
Data source	Sources of information about conditions being measured	Exit interview of students and volunteers
Applied to	The specific group within an audience to be measured (all or a subset)	Freshman taking history research module
Data interval	When data will be collected	During library orientation assignment
Target (Goal)	The amount of impact desired	85% of approximately 125 participants will self-report successful use of the library catalog; 80% of volunteers can identify specific ways they helped students use the library catalog

Source: Adapted from Leslie Edmonds Holt and Glen E. Holt, *Public Library Services for the Poor: Doing All We Can* (Chicago: American Library Association, 2010), 136.

If volunteers address envelopes, but make too many errors, you might need better training, better supervision, different volunteers, or to contract for mailing with a commercial vendor. The point is that it is important to systematically and honestly assess how volunteer jobs are done and use this information to refine or eliminate the jobs you have volunteers do in your library. Table 6.3 provides a draft example of outcome planning.

Finding Evidence That Your Volunteer Program Is Successful

A key to ongoing success of your volunteer program is regular evaluation and assessment. Generally, you should evaluate the volunteer program regularly and assess the performance of individual volunteers at appropriate intervals. Most libraries are not in a position to do formal research, though it may be possible to find funds to pay for rigorous academic research on the strength and weakness of your library volunteers. Rather, most libraries can and should institute systematic review of the volunteer program, and this review should be used to improve and plan the program in the future. Otherwise, how will you know if your volunteer program is successful? And, how will you convince library funders and the volunteers themselves that the program is successful and worth continuing?

Most volunteer programs keep a count of activity. Such things as how many volunteers the library has, how many hours the volunteers give, the monetary value of these hours, and some number amount of what volunteers accomplished (number of programs presented, books shelved, money raised) are fairly standard and reasonably easy to collect accurately. (See Chapter 8 to find out more about Volunteer Management Information Systems.) These outputs give a good idea of what volunteers did, but they really don't clarify the value of the work done, nor do they give you much information about the quality or impact of your volunteer program.

For example, you might have a count of the number of docent-led tours of the library that volunteers provided in a year. It would helpful to know how many people took these tours and whether those people liked the tour, or learned something on the tour, or had a more positive attitude toward the library because of the tour. Without going this extra step to get user input, you can't be sure of the impact of the docent tours. User input will also allow you to adjust the tours to better meet the needs and abilities of those on the tours.

So, what's the best method of evaluation for your volunteer program? There are a number of options to consider.

MEASURING VOLUNTEER PROGRAM IMPACT

Outcome planning was introduced earlier as a way to set goals for your volunteer program and to measure the extent to which those goals are met. Techniques to measure progress toward your goals may be statistical—that is, counting people, things, or activities and comparing the change in numbers over a set time period. Or you may also need to collect qualitative data that measures how people feel what attitudes they have or how they behave. Generally you will use both statistical and qualitative techniques to measure your successes and get information on how to strengthen weaknesses in your volunteer program.

According to IMLS, outcomes are:

[B]enefits to people: specifically, achievements or changes in skill, knowledge, attitude, behavior, condition, or life status for program participants ("visitors will know what architecture contributes to their environments," "participant literacy will improve"). Any project intended to create these kinds of benefits has outcome goals. Outcome-based evaluation, "OBE," is the measurement of results. . . . It systematically collects information about these indicators, and uses that information to show the extent to which a program achieved its goals. Outcome measurement differs in some ways from traditional methods of evaluating and reporting the many activities of museums and libraries, but we believe grantees will find that it helps communicate the value and quality of their work to many different audiences.[18]

In Table 6.4, you see that outcomes should be observable behaviors or characteristics of the group or groups of people involved in your volunteer program.

Table 6.4

Types of Outcomes

Attitude	What someone feels or thinks about something (e.g., to like, to be satisfied, to value . . .)
Skill	What someone can do (e.g., log on to a computer, format a word-processed document, read . . .)
Knowledge	What someone knows (e.g., the symptoms of diabetes, the state capitals, how to use a dictionary . . .)
Behavior	How someone acts (e.g., listens to others in a group, reads to children, votes . . .)
Status	Someone's social or professional condition (e.g., registered voter, high school graduate, employed . . .)
Life Condition	Someone's physical condition (e.g., nonsmoker, overweight, cancer-free . . .)

Source: From "Frequently Asked OBE Questions," Institute for Museum and Library Services, http://www.imls.gov (accessed February 2009).

You might have outcomes related to the volunteers themselves, or related to library staff or library users. You collect information from these groups directly to see what changes have come about either in your volunteer program or for library users.

Techniques to measure progress toward your goals may be statistical. For example, a goal might be to increase the number of volunteers who have computer skills. After you have defined what computer skills you need and how you will know if volunteers have these skills, simple math will allow you to measure how you are doing. You would simply need to count how many computer volunteers you have at the beginning of your recruitment drive to serve as the baseline to measure against; then, at set intervals—a month, a quarter, a year—you would take a count of the number of active computer volunteers and compare it to the baseline. If the result shows growth, you are moving in the right direction. If you have lost volunteers, it means you need to gather more information to find out why. These findings should be reported in your annual report.

There also is qualitative assessment, which helps you find out how useful your volunteer program is to the library users, to library staff, or to the volunteers themselves. Consider using it to measure the impact of your volunteer program on the larger community, in your school, or in the university.

The only sources of data about the quality of your volunteer program are the people involved in it. The idea of this kind of evaluation is really quite simple. To find out how your volunteer program is doing or how close you are to meeting your goals, you need to ask the people involved. However, the execution of this kind of evaluation is complicated. It takes care and practice to design clear, unbiased questions that pertain directly to what you want to know. Some libraries that have access to market researchers and statisticians also demand rigor in the mathematical analysis of qualitative assessment. Most libraries, however, will choose to be careful and systematic in measuring the quality and impact of their volunteer program. Many universities have a survey research center that can consult (for a fee) on how to construct interview, questionnaire, or focus group questions.

There are several ways to gather qualitative data. Volunteers can be interviewed, surveyed with written questionnaires, or observed as they do their work. Or you might chose to get feedback from volunteers or library users by using focus group discussions. The key to each of these information-gathering techniques is the careful construction of questions that produce answers that can be tabulated or summarized and used to improve your volunteer program.

If you want to learn more about the mechanics of qualitative evaluation, consult one of the following sources:

Applegate, Rachel. *Practical Evaluation Techniques for Librarians*. Santa Barbara, CA: Libraries Unlimited, 2013.

Durrance, Joan, and Fisher, Karen. *How Libraries and Librarians Help People: A Guide to Developing User-Centered Outcomes*. Chicago: American Library Association, 2005.

Elliott, Donald S., et al. *Measuring Your Library's Value: How to Do a Cost-Benefit Analysis for Your Public Library*. Chicago: American Library Association, 2007.

Hernon, Peter, Robert Dugan, and Joseph R. Mathews, *Getting Started with Evaluation*. Chicago: American Library Association, 2013.

Nelson, Sandra. *Implementing for Results: Your Strategic Plan in Action*. Chicago: American Library Association, 2009.

Owen, Patricia. *A 21st-Century Approach to School Librarian Evaluation*. Chicago: AASL, a division of the American Library Association, 2012.

WebJunction (http://www.webjunction.org) has several course offerings on evaluation and measurement.

USING EVALUATION RESULTS

Whatever method you use to evaluate your volunteer program, be sure to develop a way to use the results to sustain and improve your program. Compile your data on an ongoing basis, and compare the finding to the expectation outline in your stated goals or outcomes. Typically, librarians prepare an annual report, and the volunteer evaluation should be included. Your library may also be required to produce monthly or quarterly reports, where you can include this information. Even if no reports are required, it is still useful to compile volunteer data annually and think about what it tells you about your program.

Of course, it is easier to deal with positive results; and it is important to share positive evaluations with the volunteers and staff, library, and school administration as well as with library users and the community. It is not just bragging to do this. It will make the value of volunteers clearer to stakeholders and should enhance volunteer recruitment. Even with overall positive results, you may find ambiguous or curious results that will suggest minor changes that would improve the volunteer program or that raises questions that can be explored by future research.

For example, you may find out that the teens really liked the end-of-summer thank-you pizza party. This would suggest this is good to include in next year's plans. But if you notice that fewer than half the teens actually attended, you may want to explore ways to increase attendance by changing the time, having a different invitation, or having additional choices of food for the rare teen who doesn't like pizza.

Not meeting your objectives is more difficult to deal with. Perhaps some objectives were met partially and some not at all. It is important that you identify the likely problems and state them clearly. Volunteers and staff often have ideas about what went wrong and how to correct mistakes, so be sure to ask for their input.

Some reasons for failure are:

- Objectives are unrealistic when compared with the practice of most library volunteer programs. An example would be to attempt to reach an objective of having 90 percent of your volunteers arrive on time.
- Objectives are unrealistic in terms of the personnel available. For example, you have all 65 student volunteers supervised by one staff person.
- Conditions have changed, making the objective unreachable. For example, the two volunteers who write the Friends newsletter have left and not been replaced, so the Friends don't get out the newsletter that reminds members of Friends meetings.
- Budget has not been sufficient to meet the objective. For example, the book sale raised only half what was expected, so there were funds to support only half the volunteers.
- Personnel—volunteers or staff did not get enough training to get their work done. Staff began supervising volunteers without an understanding of the work they were to do, or volunteers were trained but did not really understand how they were to get their job done.

Most likely, if you do not fully meet your goals, your evaluation will give you good information on what didn't work. And this information will also suggest how the problems can be solved and goals met in the future.

REPORTING OUTCOMES

As well as reporting the results of your outcome evaluation internally, remember to share how your volunteer program has had an impact to the community, school, or university you serve. You don't need to share problems externally, but positive outcomes, and positive cost-benefit results, are of interest to those you serve and those who govern the library as well as the volunteers themselves.

Charlotte Mecklenburg Library acknowledges the outcomes or impacts of its volunteer program. Here's the language that CML uses to introduce its volunteer program opportunities to the potential volunteer who arrives at its website. Note how quickly the opportunities are identified as being available at the region's largest public library:

A Great Story Needs Great Characters:
Volunteer At Your Public Library
And Discover Your Power To Make A Difference

The Library owes a debt of gratitude to the many volunteers who have come forth in recent years to help us provide a steady level of service. We have seen clearly how volunteer support is essential to sustain operational effectiveness and the impact of this very committed force of library stakeholders. . . .

The caring power of our volunteers improves lives by making our libraries better. Volunteers contribute by shelving books, processing holds, leading computer classes, taking books to home bound individuals, assisting students with homework, preparing Spanish story telling sessions—all of which ultimately builds our capacity to create a more educated and literate community.

We invite you to make a difference by sharing your skills and experiences. We would like to direct you toward our most common needs which are the volunteer opportunities you see posted below. However, if you have unique skill sets please complete the *General Online Application*. We will try to find a match for you.[19]

CML's list of available volunteer opportunities describes 14 different jobs. This library's willingness to work with other potential library volunteers to find them positions within the volunteer ranks seems a bit unusual but not sufficient to limit its potential validity. The language in the CML paragraphs demonstrates that recruiting volunteers is not only about the work done, but also about building relationships and making an impact on volunteers and the community served. It is an effort to strengthen the attachment of users and nonusers alike and to confirm their value.

There are all sorts of library volunteer programs. They vary in size and complexity as well as how they are managed and supported. But all volunteer programs will work better, be sustained over time, and be more satisfying to the volunteers and those helped by volunteers if some planning is involved in administrating them. At the very least, setting goals, deciding the parameters of the volunteer program, and evaluating the program at regular intervals will help get the most out of the resources that are available. Whether the library has 10 volunteers doing one job for the library or hundreds of volunteers doing several jobs, the library will be best served with plans, procedures, and evaluation that inform decision making.

ASSESSING INDIVIDUAL VOLUNTEERS

Part of the volunteer program is assessment of individual volunteers. Many libraries find it useful to assess individual volunteers on a regular basis. This can be analogous to a performance review done for staff or an informal conversation with a volunteer after he or she has had a chance to be trained and has begun to work. The timing of the evaluation and its extent depends on how long the volunteer commitment is and how complicated the task done by the volunteer.

According to Driggers and Dumas, there are several reasons to evaluate individual volunteer performance. These are to do the following:

- Provide feedback (to individuals or groups) about the tasks performances and meeting standards.
- Learn about the volunteer's experience and feelings about the volunteer service program.
- Develop positive comments about a volunteer for use in a recognition program.
- Explore new jobs in the library that may be more suitable to an individual's skills or interests.[20]

Most volunteer appraisals can be conversational, a positive way to learn about the volunteer's experience, and reinforcement of motivation to do a good job. Some libraries have a checklist that can help focus on what the volunteer does well and what needs improvement. This list might include both general work behavior, such as "gets to work on time," or "communicates well with library users," as well as job-specific items such as accuracy of data entry or skill at leading a docent's tour of the building.

Some libraries do volunteer appraisals once a year. Usually, if there is no problem with the volunteer, the staff person who most often supervises a volunteer will do the appraisal, talk to the volunteer about it, and forward the appraisal and comments to the volunteer supervisor. Appraisals can and should be short; anything else would be costly in staff and volunteer time. Volunteers should be told about how the appraisals work when they begin at the library, so they are not surprised or put off when the appraisal is done.

If the library has short-term volunteers, people who give service for less than one month or participate in one-time volunteer activities, the library might have a short exit interview to check what the volunteer got done, how they felt about the experience, and how useful the staff supervisor thought the volunteer was. This will allow the library to improve short-term volunteer experiences and to schedule more if successful or fewer such opportunities if they are not useful.

PROBLEM VOLUNTEERS

The best thing to do with a problem volunteer is to solve the problem and keep the volunteer. There are several ways that volunteers can cause problems. Some volunteers don't have the skill or the interest to do the work you need. Others are overcommitted, don't have good transportation, or lack the physical stamina to do the work. Some volunteers have a bad attitude and/or won't take supervision. Some volunteers are rude or shy or lacking in communication skills, so they don't do well with library users or library staff. This can result in sloppy work, slow work with low productivity, inconsistent performance, and disrespectful or rude behavior.

While occasionally you might have a volunteer who has these problems, many volunteer problems can be solved by positive reinforcement, good training (or retraining), and regular positive communication with staff. Staff should talk with the volunteer, if there are problems, to try to find the cause and enlist the volunteer's help in solving the problem. Follow up with the volunteer to ensure progress.

Staff need to remind volunteers of library and volunteer rules as well as expectations for individual volunteers. If problems continue, the staff supervisor should keep a record of dates, times, and the nature of the problems, so that further discussions with volunteers can be specific and accurate. Often, if volunteers continue to have problems, they will simply stop volunteering or ask to volunteer in another department or with a different supervisor. Be careful about moving volunteers around to solve the problem; the move may not really solve anything, and even more staff time is taken up while the volunteer really doesn't improve.

Sometimes individuals have to be asked to stop volunteering at your library. This is never easy but may be very necessary. Part of your planning for your volunteer program should include reasons the volunteer will be asked to leave. Here are some examples:

- Breaking library rules
- Breaking local, state, or federal laws
- Bad attendance, late too often
- Unable, physically or mentally, to do the tasks assigned
- Won't be supervised, doesn't follow direction
- Lack of social skills or communication skills

You should also understand the laws that govern volunteers (see Chapter 4 about whistle-blowers and liability issues). This should be a part of the volunteer handbook, if you have one, and should be part of all volunteer staff orientations.

Most libraries have actual rules or informal practice about how many warnings a volunteer will get to correct behavior before they are asked to leave. The process may vary depending on the problem, but the rules should be enforced uniformly by library staff for each volunteer. For example, if students need to have a "B" average to volunteer in the school library, then all students with lower than a "B" average should be excluded from the library volunteers. Or if volunteers are dismissed after they have three unexcused absences, then all volunteers with three absences should be let go.

As with any disciplinary action, letting a volunteer go must be done in private. The volunteer supervisor should list out what the problems are and plan what to say to the volunteer. It will be helpful to have another staff member present, and it is important to be clear if the volunteer will get credit for any volunteer hours and whether and under what circumstances they might be allowed to volunteer at the library at another time. If appropriate, thank the individual for trying to be a volunteer.

Assessment is important to the volunteer program because it gives systematic, unbiased information that will help the volunteer program stay healthy and grow. If you are serious about wanting your volunteer program to be efficient and successful, it is essential to have an evaluation plan in place. This plan needs to be as simple as possible and to give you accurate information you can act on. Staff and the volunteers themselves should be involved in evaluating the volunteer program in a systematic way. You need to go beyond anecdotes of happy volunteers and look carefully to see if the program as a whole is doing what the library needs. That is, how do volunteers move the library forward? As the economist Milton Friedman said, "One of the great mistakes is to judge policies and programs by their intentions rather than their results."[21]

NOTES

1. The cited quote appeared in a virtual press release that arrived through Yahoo! The text for the release was drawn from Change Management Learning Center, "Change vs. Change Management: What Is the Difference and Why Does It Matter?" http://www.change-management.com/tutorial-change-vs-change-management.htm (accessed March 26, 2013).

2. Reimagining Service, "If We Build It, They Will Come: The Imperative for Strengthening the Nation's Volunteer Infrastructure," http://www.reimaginingservice.org/sites/default/files/u17/POL_Vol_Generation_Fund.pdf (accessed June 24, 2013).

3. Carla Land, "Dollars and Sense #18: Making the Most of Volunteers," posted December 18, 2009, http://yalsa.ala.org/blog/2009/12/18/dollars-and-sense-18-making-the-most-of-volunteers/ (accessed July 1, 2011).

4. Glen E. Holt, "Training, A Library Imperative," *Journal of Library Administration* 29, no. 1 (2000): 79–93; Glen E. Holt, "Staff Training: How Much Is Enough?" *Bottom Line* 9, no. 1 (1996): 43–44.

5. Despina Wilson, *Improving Current Processes of Assessment to Achieve Quality Goals and Outcomes* (Wilmington, DE: Wilmington College, MA-MSM, 2003), 36.

6. CASA, *A Guide to Program Development*, http://nc.casaforchildren.org/apps/annual report2012/programs.asp (accessed June 23, 2013).

7. Catholic Relief Services, *CRS Guide to Working with Volunteers* (Baltimore: Catholic Relief Services, 2012), 30. http://www.crsprogramquality.org/storage/hiv-and-aids/CRS _Guide_to_working_with_volunteers.pdf. (accessed January 7, 2013).

8. Cheyenne Mountain Zoo, "Group Volunteers," http://www.cmzoo.org/getInvolved/volunteer/groupVolunteers.asp (accessed January 7, 2013).

9. "Calif. Animal Park Reopens after Fatal Lion Attack," March 10, 2013, http://www.usatoday.com/story/news/nation/2013/03/10/animal-park-reopens/1977037/ (accessed March 13, 2013). The two earlier versions of this story appeared in television news stories on Channel 7, CBS News, Seattle, March 10 and 11.

10. Karen Beach, "Volunteer Utilization Report Prepared for Future of the Library Task Force of the Charlotte Mecklenberg Library, 2010," *Public Library Quarterly* 32, no. 2 (2013): 150–62.

11. Mark A. Hager and Jeffrey L. Brudney, *Balancing Act: The Challenges and Benefits of Volunteers* (Washington, DC: Urban Institute, 2004), 1, http://www.urban.org/UploadedPDF/411125_balancing_act.pdf (accessed May 27, 2009).

12. Donald Elliott, Glen E. Holt, Sterling Hayden, and Leslie Edmonds Holt, *Measuring Your Library's Value: How to Do a Cost-Benefit Analysis for Your Public Library* (Chicago: ALA Editions, 2006).

13. Hager and Brudney, *Balancing Act*, 1.

14. Ibid., 12.

15. Beach, "Volunteer Utilization Report."

16. Ibid.

17. Independent Sector, "Independent Sector's Value of Volunteer Time," http://www.independentsector.org/volunteer_time (accessed May 13, 2013).

18. IMLS, "Outcome Based Evaluation: The Basics," http://www.imls.gov/applicants/basics.aspx (accessed May 2, 2013).

19. Charlotte Mecklenburg Library, Volunteer Program Recruitment page, http://www.cmlibrary.org/about_us/get_involved/volunteer.asp (accessed January 8, 2013).

20. Preston Diggers and Eileen Dumas, *Managing Library Volunteers*, 2nd ed. (Chicago: American Library Association, 2011), 225.

21. http://www.goodreads.com/quotes/search?utf8=%E2%9C%93&q=friedman&commit=Search (accessed May 1, 2013).

7

Volunteers That Require Special Attention

Like all books, this one is written at a specific level of generality: It offers advice and direction about how to organize and operate a successful, high-impact volunteer program in your library. All sorts of librarians can use these suggestions to improve the quality of their volunteer programs. However, a few kinds of volunteer programs need special attention from library managers to make them work well and thrive.

FRIENDS OF THE LIBRARY

One of these programs is Library Friends. All types of libraries have Friends groups. They are distinct from other volunteer activities because they have members (often with a membership fee), are usually governed by Friends members, and actively raise funds for the parent library. Friends of libraries constitute a voluntary aspect of library life that deserves special attention because as a group, formal Friends, usually designated by the capital "F" on their name, create special opportunities for the library.

Benefits

On the plus side, Friends groups have undertaken many projects that make them eligible to fit into the various exemplar categories presented to readers in Chapters 2 and 3. They have organized libraries, funded libraries, and advocated for libraries in the community as well as with governing agencies (such as school boards, university boards of regents, or city councils). They also have carried out numerous special projects that have brought prestige, revenue, and more Friends members. Successful Friends engage the community, run book sales, and spread good stories about why your library is important and a source of pride to those served and to the community generally. They are well worth the time and effort that library administrators need to allocate to make them successful.

The American Library Association and United for Libraries (formerly Friends of Libraries USA) strongly recommend that all Friends groups follow best practices for raising and handling money, and that they be constituted with a mission statement and a workable organizational structure.

Friends and Foundations

If they are going to handle money, or operate within or for your library, encourage your Friends to register as a 501(c)(3) nonprofit organization. This IRS legal status prevents the Friends group from having to pay taxes and allows donors to make their gifts with a legitimate, maximum tax deduction.[1] That status is useful, although some publicly funded libraries have experienced considerable difficulty obtaining 501(c)(3) status from the IRS

Remember, though, that a publicly funded library almost always can set up a not-for-profit foundation for various purposes, including fund-raising. No matter what the library's size or purpose, be careful if you already have a 501(c)(3) foundation, and your group, which is chartered as a 501(c)(3), decides to set up another 501(c)(3) foundation. Inevitably, this multiplicity of Friends and more than one foundation transforms into competitive and often ineffective fund-raising on behalf of the library.

What Do Friends Groups Do?

Here are some positive examples of what Friends groups have done for libraries over the years.

The Elkins Park (Pennsylvania) Library Friends organized and created the modern library in 1957, including raising a new and larger building and furnishing it with $157,000 of interior materials.[2] Other achievements include providing family programs, materials delivery to the homebound, and art exhibits in the library. They also publish a newsletter and raise money for new books and magazines.[3]

The Elkins Park achievements on behalf of their library did not stop with these activities. There came a moment when the library was in dire need of a spring cleaning, so the Friends of the Elkins Park Library utilized their board's volunteer energy for their first Annual "Rag Day" event. Members who looked the sloppiest before and the dirtiest afterwards received prizes—certificates good for 10 free used books from the sale shelves. The event ended with pizza. For public relations, the Friends sent to media outlets photos of everyone mopping, dusting, and scrubbing. And, their accounts claim that "Rag Day" didn't just spruce up the library, it also helped to solidify the library's board.[4]

The Friends of the Oboler Library at Idaho State University was organized in 2003. The organization's membership is drawn from both the university and civic organizations. The organization is known as "FOOL" (*Friends Of Oboler Library*) after the medieval jester who with "impunity speaks truth to power." In keeping with this theme, FOOL supports programs on intellectual and academic freedom that honor local, regional, and national authors. FOOL also raises funds to support its programs.[5]

The theme of the Friends of the Oakland Public School Libraries (FOPSL) is that every child deserves a quality school library. Since 2009, 12 libraries have been completely renovated or restored with the help of community volunteers from the Friends. FOPSL also provides storytimes and other programs.[6]

For information on starting or operating a Friends group, ALA has several useful publications. See the box below.

Here are the 27 ALA titles of fact sheets for Friends groups and library foundations.

1. How to Organize a Friends Group
2. Fund-Raising Campaigns
3. A Checklist for Planning Successful Programs
4. How to Organize an Academic Friends Group
5. How to Organize a Teen Friends of the Library Group
6. How to Organize a Friends of a School Library Group
7. How to Revitalize Your Friends Group
8. Getting Involved with Literacy Programs
9. Planning a Book and Author Event
10. The Role of the Friends Board
11. The Role of Library Trustees
12. Designating a Literary Landmark
13. Checklist for Advocacy
14. Friends Board Development
15. Moving to Center Stage in the Community and on Campus
16. How to Organize a Foundation
17. Getting and Keeping Members
18. Branch Friends of the Library
19. A Checklist for Friends Board Strategic Planning
20. Friends Board Diversity
21. State Friends
22. Guidelines for Giving
23. Advocacy Campaigns: Legal Limits on Spending for Nonprofits
24. Planned Giving: What You Need to Know
25. Sample Memorandum of Understanding
26. Library Support for Friends Activities
27. When Friends Aren't Friendly

Concerns

One of the most useful ALA documents concerning Friends is the one entitled "When Friends Aren't Friendly," which clarifies some of the problems that can arise with Friends groups. Here is a summary: Most Friends groups are indispensable to the libraries they serve. Sadly, though, some Friends groups get out of sync with their library, their mission, and their roles. When this kind of trouble happens, trust and goodwill evaporate and relationships break down.[7] Typically problems arise because Friends are unwilling (or unable) to share financial information with library administration, or the group wants to spend its money independently from the library; the Friends don't communicate with library administration, actively or publicly oppose library staff decisions, or operate like an exclusive club with the leadership never changing.

How to Help Friends Help the Library

Nearly always the problems that Friends cause in and for libraries are because they act independently from the library's organizational life and culture. Your library can minimize the problems it will have with its Friends by following a set of operational rules.

Start with a clear understanding of the mission and operational procedures for your Friends—and put it in writing. These include:

- Firm understanding of what the friends will do.
- Firm understanding of what resources the library will provide to them.
- Publicity, credit, and recognition of their successful activity that the library will provide.
- Regular formal communication. Someone from high in administration needs to meet with the Friends' decision-makers and attend friends meetings on a regular basis.
- In some circumstances, a de facto or actual contract regarding resources and operational policies might be signed by the leadership of the Friends, the library's governing officials or board executives, and the director.
- Evaluation should be similar to the library's internal annual evaluation. Every director ought to regularly examine what and how friends are operating as part of regular critical organizational analyses. At the very least, Friends need evaluation on how they match library purposes, programs, and products.
- Training of Friends leaders, similar to training of staff and/or training of volunteers.
- Keep track of the value of Friends' time and resource contributions. The Friends need to use acceptable accounting standards and be audited regularly.
- Have a long-term Friends plan that includes how new Friends will be recruited and how new leaders will be selected. Encourage term limits for Friends leaders.

Libraries can be enriched by having a friends group that contributes funds, workers and support. As ALA states, "Libraries need Friends—now more than ever. They need Friends who are positive about the library and its direction, who understand their important role for fundraising and advocacy, and who stick to their mission to support the library."[8]

YOUTH VOLUNTEERS

Many public and school libraries have children and teen volunteers. Any library might have young people become a part of the regular volunteer program. As with any volunteer group, the library's youth volunteers should have goals and outcomes, along with a clear sense of how supervision, evaluation, and recognition will occur.

Benefits

As with other volunteers, children and teens can help the library meet its goals and get work done. Young people may be happy to do repetitive tasks, such as cutting out name tags for storytime or making sure books and materials get checked out correctly. This volunteer effort saves staff time for other, more complicated work.

Young people who volunteer at the library can be excellent ambassadors to other young people. Youth volunteers can invite their friends and classmates to use the library or to attend a specific program at the library. Student volunteers can help other children or teens understand the rules and procedures for using the school library sometimes more effectively than library staff, as they speak peer to peer and might be both clearer and more persuasive than an adult.

Who Are Youth Volunteers?

Each library needs to define the ages and other factors that qualify youth for its volunteer program. Most school libraries draw from their own student body, though each may have a reason to limit the grade or age of volunteers. Many elementary schools, for instance, allow only fourth and fifth grade students who have a good academic record to volunteer. Public libraries can choose any age to be included, though most pick teens.

In addition to the age of volunteers, consider how your volunteer program can best serve the young people volunteering, the library, and the library users. Librarian Kellie Gillespie, who works in this field, writes that teens often volunteer to meet some need. These include fulfillment of a community service requirement, as a positive factor in college admission, to gain work experience, to improve their community, to fulfill a desire for social experience, to fill time constructively, to feel a sense of accomplishment and, still more simply, to have a safe place to hang out.[9]

One thing children who use the library may get from seeing young volunteers in the library is a sense that the library is a welcoming place. While the authors of this book worked at St. Louis Public Library, they began a teen volunteer group, in part, because grade school children told us that they liked the library staff, but that they were too old. The kids "knew" the library was for preschoolers and thought the place might be too babyish for them. Adding teen volunteers after school and in the summer changed the attitude of grade-schoolers, and they reported feeling welcome and stopped commenting on the age of the staff. Over time, SLPL teen volunteers also became more racially and linguistically diverse, so children saw kids "like me" when they visited the library.

The library's goals for volunteers often are task-driven—books to be shelved; children to be mentored, tutored, or read to; clerical tasks to be completed; or just an extra pair of hands at an open house or party. To create a successful youth volunteer program, the librarian needs to recognize and design one that meets the needs of the volunteers, the library, and its users.

What Do Youth Volunteers Do?

Here are some examples of how libraries use young volunteers.

Carver County Library in Minnesota welcomes teens as volunteers. Staff tell teens that "volunteering at the library is a great way to serve your community and gain work experience. Teen volunteers can help the library and count their hours for school, scouting, or other community service projects."[10] Carver County Library offers a wide variety of opportunities from which teens can choose, and training is provided. Teens help with summer reading program activities, help shelve and shelf read, empty the bookdrop, hunt for reserve materials, work at assigned clerical tasks, and assist in preschool storytimes. Bilingual teens help translate for library users who need it.[11]

The Allen Elementary School Library in Ann Arbor, Michigan, recruits student volunteers for its Library Squad. The Library Squad is the student body's contribution to the behind-the-scenes work that makes the library run. Being a Squad member means you're doing important, essential work to help the entire school community. Library Squad members work at lunch time once a week. Squad members shelve books, collect materials from classrooms, attach bar codes and labels, and perform other tasks when needed.[12]

The Prairie Point Middle School and Ninth Grade Academy Library in Cedar Rapids, Iowa, recruits students who are interested in working with students and staff in an educational setting; who want experience with and knowledge of library organization. Computer experience is essential. The job description for volunteers notes that they assist the teacher librarian and library paraprofessional by:

- Helping create displays, bulletin boards, and announcements.
- Performing clerical duties (i.e., typing, covering/repairing books).
- Sorting and reshelving library materials.
- Performing other duties as assigned by the teacher librarian and the library paraprofessional.[13]

Concerns

There are several concerns when working with young volunteers. These include:

- Developmental limitations. Younger children have limited skills (remember, alphabetizing is an upper-level skill) and limited attention spans. Teens may have the needed skills, but may become easily bored.
- Young volunteers may have limited social experience and need to learn volunteer etiquette. This might include being polite, arriving on time, dressing appropriately, and following library rules.
- Your city or state may have child labor laws that limit how long and what time of day young people can work. While volunteering is not work, it is wise to use established rules

as guidelines. The U.S. Department of Labor has information on rules for child labor by state at http://www.dol.gov/dol/location.htm. Cities or counties may also have rules. Even when children aren't being paid, there may be regulations about how long they can work or working in the evening. Often these rules apply to anyone under the age of 16.

- Most young volunteers don't have their own transportation, so they may not be reliable. Also, the younger the volunteer, the more likely parents or others control their time. Parents may need their children to babysit or decide that a family excursion is more important than their child's volunteer obligations.
- Children and teens who are fulfilling school, scout, or church service requirements may have little or no real interest in the library or the work you ask them to do.
- Young volunteers may require or request more paperwork from you—forms or letters of recommendation to get jobs, get into college, or meet school requirements.
- Young volunteers need more supervision than adult volunteers and should not volunteer alone with staff (or older youth volunteers).
- Young volunteers may be much more interested in socializing with other volunteers rather than getting work done. Or the opposite—they are very shy or hostile and don't want to work with others.

How to Run a Successful Youth Volunteer Program

With some planning and flexibility, any library can have a successful student or teen volunteer program that meets both the volunteer's and library's needs.

Before you start, do your homework. Find out about the service requirements for young people in your community or school. Talk to kids about their interest in volunteering, and find out what times would work for them. If you have a way to talk to parents, find out their ideas about their children or teens volunteering. Talk to librarians who have successful volunteer programs to learn the "dos and don'ts" and about how much time staff is needed to operate a youth volunteer program.

Second, form a plan. What do you want to accomplish by having a teen volunteer program? How many kids can you manage in the program? What jobs will they do? What about recommendations and recognition? In St. Louis, we viewed our teen volunteers as an important middle school program. It was run to benefit 12- to 16-year-olds who needed work experience and career education as well as a way to attract these young teens to the library. That the library and the librarians received much-needed help was an added benefit but not the primary reason for the program. Your library may have other reasons to have youth volunteers, such as resume building for older teens, a way to offer more programs to the community, confidence-building for younger children, or a way to relieve staff from clerical duties.

Third, figure out how you will recruit teen volunteers. How will kids find out about the program? Who is eligible? What is the application process? How often will you recruit (e.g., the beginning of each semester or during the summer only)? Will you have workdays in which all kids have to do is show up?

Fourth, set rules that are appropriate to the young people in your program. For example, SLPL staff found that young people were more comfortable working in pairs, but more than two or three at once was too much. Children and teens should do their work in the public area or with several people in a work area. Let them know they need to call the library if they are not going to work at the appointed time; and that three missed workdays means they are out of the program. School libraries may also have rules about volunteers needing to maintain good grades.

Fifth, train staff (or adult volunteers) who will work with young volunteers. In addition to learning how the youth volunteer program works, they will need some reminders on communicating with children or teens. Figure out how best to supervise young volunteers. Teen volunteers need someone to report to every time they volunteer. It is good if it is the same person every time, but be realistic about how to cover if a staff person is ill or schedules change. Let staff know how much time they should be spending with each volunteer. You might tell them that staff should take 10 minutes per hour with each volunteer or pair of volunteers if they are learning a new task, but five minutes if they are doing something they have already learned to do.

Lastly, figure out how you are going to thank youth volunteers, if you are going to write individual recommendations or have a form letter, and what other benefits young volunteers might realize. A pizza party might be a great "thank you," or a library T-shirt might be appreciated. Do teen volunteers get tours of behind the scenes operations of the library or receive special invitations to meet a visiting author? Do you offer programs on using library resources to apply for college or to apply for a job?

Make sure you evaluate the kids and the program on a regular basis. Ask the volunteers, their parents, library staff (and teachers), and, if possible, library users what works about the program and what doesn't. Then use this information to improve the program for the next round of youth volunteers.

Working with elementary, middle, and high school people may be an acquired taste, but if done right, it is a win-win situation. The library gets help, attracts young users, and provides the community or school with an opportunity for service. And the kids get work experience, positive contact with adults, other teens and often younger children. Try it, you'll like it!

PERSONS WITH DISABILITIES

In 2010, ASCLA issued a useful tip sheet on how libraries can become more engaged with persons with disabilities. ASCLA points out that such persons do not "necessarily have the same opportunities to volunteer because of intentional or unintentional community barriers." The tip sheet continues, "If you can position your library as the go-to place for potential volunteers with disabilities, you may find a substantial and consistent source of volunteers. Remember, reading, walking, talking, and so forth are not necessarily requirements for the volunteer job."[14]

That admonition includes developmentally disabled. A decade ago, Kathryn Purdon wrote a very informative article suggesting the reasons why developmentally disabled persons were a good choice for volunteer programs. In the article, she was adamant that such persons were not discriminated against by the institutions where they were volunteered, being treated as persons without knowledge, ability, or the sense to know when they were being mistreated. There certainly is a place for developmentally disabled persons among library volunteers, including work in library jobs that will provide experience that might lead to social and economic advancement.[15]

PARTNERSHIP VOLUNTEERS

You may have the opportunity to work with other agencies to get volunteers for your library. This might include scout troops, church groups, and service organizations such as the Lions, United Way, or service groups from schools and universities. Also the chamber of commerce, retired workers, unions, the military, or agencies serving older adults, developmentally or otherwise disabled people, veterans, or low-income people may offer to bring groups to volunteer at the library. You may also have the opportunity to work with unpaid interns or student teachers who get academic credit for their work at your library. You also may qualify to get workers paid by a third party, but with little or no salary cost to you. This might include AmeriCorps, various job-training programs including Welfare to Work or academic programs that allow students to do research at your library. And last, but not least, workers may be supplied by the court system to do community service.

While each partnership has to be arranged for and managed on its own, there are some universal organizing principles that may help to forge successful experiences for the library, the volunteers, and the partners.

Benefits of Volunteer Partnerships

There is a Maori proverb that says "with my resources and your resources everyone will benefit."[16] This is the reason to seek out partners for your volunteer program.

The biggest benefit to working with other agencies to recruit and use volunteers for your library is that you get some help from another agency or group to achieve your library's goals. Maybe you use the United Way to recruit volunteers by using their volunteer job website, or the scout leader comes with a group of girls and supervises them as they clean books or read to younger children. Or, for another example, perhaps a group of retired tech workers volunteer to develop training for seniors so they can better use the library's Internet connection.

Another benefit is that partners may help you recruit volunteers that are difficult to find. These include volunteers that need professional-level skills or specific qualifications, like those of businesspeople, students, or academics. It also includes volunteers that will do jobs that other volunteers don't want to do, such as moving furniture, sorting books for a book sale, or doing yard work. Often groups are willing to help out during a one-time workday for a service group. Most court-ordered volunteers find working in a library setting more rewarding than picking up trash along the highway.

Lastly, by using volunteers from partner agencies, you may get volunteers who are not familiar with the library to visit and learn about what you do. In addition, these volunteers may develop some ownership of your library after they have worked to improve it in some way. Sometimes volunteers who work at the library for a day with their church or service group will be interested in joining the library volunteer program on a continuing basis.

What Kinds of Partnership Volunteers Are There?

Third-party agencies work with libraries in a variety of ways. Sometimes work is provided occasionally, with volunteers being recruited for one-day or short-term commitments; and sometimes volunteer work is ongoing. Here are some examples.

Judevine Center for Autism and the St. Louis Public Library worked out an effective volunteer-use partnership. Judevine provided job training and employment for adults with autism (among other services). For many years, Judevine would bring small groups of these adults to the St. Louis Public Library to prepare mailings of library newsletters and other clerical projects. Judevine staff trained their clients and supervised their work. The library provided space, a staff person to organize and supervise the work, and snacks. Judevine volunteers got real work training; they had an opportunity to work in a noninstitutional setting; and the library got its mailings done cheaply and quickly.

The Salt Lake County Public Library developed a successful program using court-ordered community service volunteers. Like Salt Lake City, many libraries accept court-ordered community service volunteers, but the courts usually require that each library and each court must work out the requirements together before starting a partnership. Considerations include who the courts will refer (what offenses), what paperwork will be required, and any literacy or education requirements the library might require. Salt Lake will consider court-mandated service for traffic offenses and truancy. All Court Ordered Volunteers are screened by the Library System Volunteer Coordinator prior to service. Court Ordered Community Service opportunities are limited. To be considered, potential volunteers have to be interviewed by the library's volunteer coordinator.[17]

The Santa Barbara, California, School Libraries also established a partnership program with Partners in Education, a nonprofit organization that seeks to connect businesses and individuals with schools and the programs that serve them. The Partners in Education program has the goal of helping improve public education in ways that support a more vibrant economy, the health of the community, and the well-being of local children and their families. As part of this effort, Partners in Education recruits volunteers for selected public school libraries. Volunteers from the program who work in the library process new books, create library displays, develop reading lists, read to and with students, and help with the end-of-the-year inventory.[18]

The library at the University of Hawai'i at Manoa hosts a Library Internship Program that instructs LIS students from the Information Studies Program of the Department of Information and Computer Science. The work is usually unpaid but wins course credit as LIS 690, an intern program designed for advanced students pursuing the MLISc degree to obtain practical preprofessional field experience to augment their academic coursework. Students work 150 hours in one semester under the direction of a library staff member as well as a faculty adviser. Interns can also work in 13 other academic libraries in the region.[19]

Concerns

Cooperative or partnership programs may come about naturally—that is, when both organizations have goals that are compatible, and the rules and procedures of each organization can be adapted to a joint program. Most partnerships, however, take some effort and flexibility to bring about both institutional cooperation and workable volunteer use. Some common issues follow:

- Volunteer skill level. If you use volunteers recruited by a third party, you may not get volunteers with the skills you need. For example, not all members of the local church guild may be equally good at reading aloud to children in the school media center.
- Scheduling volunteers. There may be challenges in getting volunteers when they're needed or can be accommodated. For example, the scout group who wants to help with library landscaping may not be available when a library staff member has time to work with them.
- Mission disconnect or conflict of interest. If potential partners have strong political, religious, or business goals, they may be incompatible with the library's values. For example, a real estate association that offers to do programs and provide individual counseling at the library would need to agree to not use these services to sell real estate.
- Added planning and administrative costs. To make a cooperative volunteer program work, there is the initial effort to identify, understand, and pilot a program between the library and the other agency. There may also be ongoing "extra" effort needed to use a special application, training protocol, or supervision that would be ongoing. Moreover, staff at the partner agency may change, so you have to work with new people often.

How to Organize a Successful Volunteer Partnership

In developing partnerships for your volunteer program, it is important to listen carefully to what the partner agency wants to accomplish, and how they manage and offer their services. Not every offer of volunteers is a good fit from your library, so feel comfortable in saying "no" to programs that are good but do not fit what you need.

Be clear about how the library volunteer program works and what either by rule or practice cannot be changed; but be flexible when you can and when it is needed to be a successful partner.

Draw up a plan with the partner on what the partnership will accomplish for your library, for the partner and for the volunteers involved. Decide the details of how the program will work—how many volunteers will be involved, how often will they work at the library, how long each work session will be, and who will supervise them. If the plans look good, pilot the partnership with a few volunteers; and then meet with the partners to troubleshoot problems and schedule how to implement an ongoing partnership. Have a written budget if appropriate and put everything in writing to avoid confusion and facilitate consistency.

Commit with the partner agency and the volunteers to evaluate the partnership regularly. Market your success with your partner within the library and in the community.

As with all aspects of library management, it is important to be open to opportunities to improve and grow your volunteer program. Not all libraries will have the opportunity to have a Friends group or youth volunteers, or to work with community partners on volunteer projects. And, not all libraries that have these opportunities should have them. If the library cannot provide the special attention needed and take the time to work with these special groups, staff should not start or continue to run such programs. However, when done carefully, each of these groups can be a true asset to the library, and librarians should be open to the possibilities that Friends, youth, or partners can bring to the library's volunteer program.

NOTES

1. American Library Association, "Ways to Advocate as a Friend," http://www.ilove libraries.org/ways-advocate-friend/ (accessed April 5, 2013).

2. Cheltenham Township Library System website, http://www.cheltenhamlibraries.org/ elkins_park/ep_friends_library_history.php (accessed November 1, 2012).

3. Ibid.

4. ALTAFF website, http://www.ala.org/ala/mgrps/divs/altaff/friends/ideasharing/ volunteers.cfm (accessed December 20, 2009).

5. Idaho State University Library, "Friends of Oboler Library," http://www.isu.edu/library/ friends (accessed April 5, 2013).

6. Friends of the Oakland Public School Libraries website, http://www.fopsl.org/ (accessed April 5, 2013).

7. American Library Association, "When Friends Aren't Friendly," http://www.ala.org/ united/sites/ala.org.united/files/content/friends/factsheets/unitedff27.pdf (accessed April 23, 2013).

8. Ibid.

9. Kellie M. Gillespie, *Teen Volunteer Services in Libraries* (Latham, MD: VOYA Books and imprint of Scarecrow Press, 2004), 11.

10. Carver County Library, "Be a Teen Volunteer," https://www.carverlib.org/SitePages/teen _volunteers.aspx (accessed April 25, 2013).

11. Ibid.

12. Allen Elementary School, "What Is the Library Squad?" http://www.a2schools.org/ allen.home/allen.mediacenter/student_volunteers__the_library_squad (accessed April 25, 2013).

13. Prairie Point Middle School, "Job Description: Student Volunteer," http:// www.pointlibrary.org/2/post/2010/09/be-a-library-student-volunteer.html (accessed April 25, 2013).

14. Association of Specialized and Cooperative Library Agencies (ASCLA). "Volunteers with Disabilities: What You Need to Know: Library Accessibility Tip Sheet 9" (Chicago: ASCLA, 2010), http://www.ala.org/ascla/sites/ala.org.ascla/files/content/asclaprotools/accessibility tipsheets/tipsheets/9-Volunteers_with_Di.pdf (accessed March 30, 2013).

15. Kathryn Purdon, "Including the Developmentally Disabled in Traditional Volunteer Programs: Why Organizations Should Do It, and How to Get There," December 2003, http:// www.serviceleader.org/instructors/studentpaper9 (accessed April 3, 2011).

16. Salt Lake City Public Library, "Library Volunteer Opportunities," http://www.slcolibrary.org/gl/glvl/ (accessed April 28, 2013).

17. Ibid.

18. Volunteer Match, "Santa Barbara Partners in Education," http://volunteermatch.org/search/org89158.jsp (accessed April 28, 2013).

19. University of Hawai'i at Manoa Library, "Library Internship Program," http://library.manoa.hawaii.edu/about/jobs.html (accessed April 28, 2013).

8

Volunteer Management Information Systems

RATIONALE FOR A VMIS

You can feel the staff change resisters getting ready to giggle as soon as this subject comes up for discussion. Their message: "We've been doing volunteers for decades. Why do we need an electronic volunteer information system now or ever?"

The rationale is simple: Better information about volunteer activity up, down, and across the organization. Many libraries have successfully kept volunteer statistics in paper form. In smaller libraries this works well, but it is easy to lose the forms, fail to gather all of them at one time, or get them mixed in with staff sign-in sheets. In larger libraries these problems are multiplied, as staff gather information from all locations to tabulate totals. That means extra work for staff. The great advantage to electronic data is that it is stored and tabulated all in one place, and anyone who needs it has access to the information. If library volunteers are not experienced using computers, most VMIS are easy to use and volunteers can be trained to enter their hours into the system.

As we have pointed out earlier in this book, volunteer activity often matches the complexity of the organization. Library volunteers, to use the old cliché, are here, there, and everywhere, engaged in activity that often varies within different work and branch units. The volunteer situation at St. Louis Public was fairly typical. Many different kinds of volunteers worked in 16 library locations, plus volunteers covered special events and did kid outreach to schools and daycare centers. An electronic Volunteer Management Information System (VMIS) helped library staff and volunteers know what volunteers were doing and access information that made management of all kinds—including placement, hours worked, and substitution, much easier to handle.

Perhaps the best evidence for using a VMIS comes from the U.S. Army, which records all of its volunteer activities (on and off base, by its military staff and by their families and residents, and businesspersons who operate around their bases) in an electronic information system. This guide for volunteers in military settings or soldiers volunteering off base includes the following types of information:

- Roles and responsibilities of volunteers
- Applications for a volunteer position
- Volunteer tools
- Record volunteer activity
- Record volunteer hours
- Add a non-Army Volunteer Corps Service
- Add an award or special recognition
- Download the Volunteer Service Record
- Edit the Volunteer Profile Information
- Edit volunteer activity
- View Volunteer Annual Summary
- Contact for Additional Assistance[1]

SOME VMIS OPTIONS

There already are options in volunteer information systems. Here are a few commercial systems that attracted our review.

Volgistics (Volunteer Logistics)

Volgistics has one of the most informative websites for VMISs.[2] A visit to the company website provides an immediate test drive of their system, letting you take a look at an anonymous operating system with the ability to track the various data that you can insert. In less than half an hour, you can learn a huge amount about the dynamics of their VMIS. One quite dynamic sales page in large letters and numbers claims that Volgistics serves 2,934 organizations, which benefits 68,018 "leaders," and their software tracks the activities of 3,381,729 volunteers on the day we visited the site. And, the numbers served changes as the date changes.

Volgistics has a software package for Libraries Volunteer Information Management. Its categories include:

- Recruiting—This includes a ready-made online application that can be tailored "to the needs of your organization." The information from completed applications is automatically transferred to your database when you accept them.
- Tracking—The library professional can save addresses, phone numbers, and e-mail addresses for emergency contacts, employers, references, and parents or guardians for each volunteer. You can also create customizable fields to track things important to your organization such as special skills or job preferences. Volgistics comes equipped with items already set up for categorical report writing.
- Service records—"A comprehensive history of service hours, dates, times, and assignments is available on each volunteer's record," with report writing capability on existent data sets.

- Communication—E-mailing and mailing label production are included in the communication sections. Mailings can be forwarded to both shows and no-shows with only one set of commands.
- Online Volunteer Portal—"Volunteers sign-in to a secure portal to download forms, schedule assignments, update contact information, receive messages and review their service. And, they can even enter their own service information, with the hours served automatically becoming part of their individual record. This can be a real time saver for busy volunteer managers!" The system manager can control the kind of information that volunteers can enter into the library system and check accuracy of data entered by volunteers.
- Recognition—There are lots of possible recognitions for hours or years served and for special awards as well.
- Multisite access—This feature makes it easy for compliance items, awards, password security settings, field formats, and more to be standardized for the entire organization. Headquarters operators can still create reports for volunteer service at all of the library system's branches. However, site-level operators see a simplified interface that limits volunteer information from being shared between locations unless a system authority allows such exchange.
- Conversion—You can convert your current volunteer data choosing the transferable method that matches your budget and the program you're using now.[3]

VolunteerHub

VolunteerHub is another vendor that offers an information system for tracking volunteers at libraries. Its page addressed to library clients categorizes its library programs under scheduling, calendar, hours tracking, database, and an ROI (Return on Investment) calculator.[4] The VolunteerHub system is worth a look, if only to see what a minimalist approach to slick graphics and information can achieve. VolunteerHub operates "in the cloud." You do not have to bother your IT folks with many setup issues.

CERVIS

CERVIS (Community Event Registration and Volunteer Information System) does not offer ready-made library software.[5] The company's offer, however, does make it easy to find out if your library can make use of the system. CERVIS offers a month-long tryout and a money-back guarantee. The website has a slick look and feel, suggesting that it can easily be morphed to any library's purposes. The company's website says, "CERVIS makes it easy to recruit volunteers online, coordinate and manage volunteer opportunities, and communicate effectively with volunteers." CERVIS charges its users a monthly fee, depending on which services the library uses.

Capterra.com

Capterra.com offers a different kind of assistance, helping you find exactly the right system for your institutional VMIS. Capterra summarizes 10 systems with the promise of helping you adapt one that will fit your particular organizational needs. The company also offers a wonderful schematic cartoon of "Your Roadmap to Buying Business Software." The linear graphic is set up like a multipage

Monopoly board, with clusters of decisions that need to be made at each stage of the adoption and installation. If you are thinking about electronic software to manage volunteers, you'll enjoy a visit, and learn a lot at Capterra.com.[6] There is no charge for using the roadmap tool.

CHOOSING THE INFORMATION YOU NEED: KCLS SELECTION LIST

Before choosing a Volunteer Management Information System for your library, think about what kind of information you want it to hold. Now, if you work in a small organization with a smaller cadre of volunteers, you may be questioning whether this chapter applies to you. The authors believe that it does; the larger, more formal—and probably more costly—information systems will provide even smaller libraries with options that they might not consider as possibilities without the efforts that some large libraries make in handling volunteer information.

It is that logic that brings us to an illustration using the King County Library System, which is featured as a library case study in the Appendix of this book. Part of KCLS planning for a big change in its volunteer program involved planning for a VMIS that would fit into the organization's articulated volunteer plan in the Appendix, you can learn about the work that went into the creation of the system's 2008–2009 volunteer program reforms. One element of that reform was working with the staff to create a VMIS that would have the capabilities to meet all the needs that staff planners anticipated in managing the reformed and expanded volunteers program.

When you read the Appendix, you will see how KCLS surveyed 200 staff members, seeking guidance about what changes were needed to bring major reform to the volunteer program. This section presents a list of data elements that staff suggested for inclusion in the library's VMIS in order to do a good job with and for volunteers.[7]

In the introduction to this survey, the library administration explained that "the purpose of the electronic software volunteer management program is to hold data to provide the essential information that staff need to manage the program and make the volunteer fill rate hold up." Staff who took the survey were asked to give a numerical ranking in one of three categories: "Required," "Desirable," or "Optional." The list serves as an excellent array of data sets that those who are trying to reform or start up their volunteer programs might consider setting up in their own in-house information system.

Here are the information categories and data sets that KCLS put before their staff if they thought the item ought to be "Required," "Desired," or "Optimal" in its usefulness. To reiterate, we are not suggesting that you should select all of these data categories, but this document offers you the opportunity to see and learn from a working document that became a finished volunteer management information system. Please note that we have changed the wording of some of these items to clarify their meaning for those not part of KCLS staff.

Data

1. All data from individual volunteer application.
2. Staff contact for this volunteer—program and branch level.

3. Status: Regular, Substitute, or Regular volunteer who will substitute.
4. Have they volunteered before at KCLS?
5. Emergency contact info.
6. Regardless of program one place for records for all volunteers.
7. Demographics; number of hours.
8. Space for staff notes—issues that are recurring.
9. Notes area; problems flagged for other staff members.
10. KCLS history available for inactive staff members.
11. Able to assign a volunteer to multiple programs and/or multiple branches.
12. Gap of when they left and are coming back.
13. Types of activities they did.
14. ID photos; publish to staff so they know who they are.
15. Date/Time stamp of each change and able to put in initials to show who made any changes to a record.
16. If affiliated with the Friends.
17. Affiliation with local service groups, such as the Blue Bills.

Automated Functionality

1. Eliminate any KCLS online application not tied to a specific opportunity. We don't want a person to apply for something that doesn't exist.
2. Auto check if they are 21 years old (for Virtual Study Zone).
3. Calculate actual anniversaries and hours worked, taking into account any leaves of absence.
4. Populate database from online application as "pending" volunteer.
5. Able to communicate with people signed up for an orientation in event it is cancelled or changed.
6. Auto switch status to adult on 18th birthday?
7. Enter KCLS holidays annually.
8. System bars staff from scheduling volunteers on a holiday.
9. Reminders to volunteers of holidays coming up. "Next Monday we are closed."
10. Online applications specific to a volunteer opportunity.
11. Able to sign up for an orientation during application process.

Scheduling

1. Who is scheduled when.
2. Able to print the daily schedule for all volunteers at a particular branch.
3. Volunteers can enter scheduling requests and when they are available to sub or work.
4. Staff prompted whether they want to send out an email for subs for that shift.

Timekeeping

1. Want to look up someone's hours, past and present.
2. Want volunteers to be able to look up their own hours.
3. Want volunteers to clock in and out only from KCLS site, not remote entry of hours worked (or entry for Outreach volunteers).

4. Timekeeping works for state requirements for labor and industry coverage.
5. Track hours volunteered over a cumulative time period—daily, weekly, monthly, yearly.
6. Keep a running total of volunteered hours for acknowledgment and appreciation—X number of hours over X years.
7. Want system to ask supervisor to verify hours.

Reports

1. Real-time reports: who is on now; where they are.
2. Active, inactive volunteers.
3. Monthly reports for management by branch, program, system.
4. Trends by branch or by program; charts showing trends in numbers of volunteers; number of volunteer hours.

Communication

1. In event of unexpected closure, able to quickly e-mail volunteers scheduled that day to notify them.
2. Reminders to volunteers of holidays coming.
3. E-mail direct from the database; create a message and send it out.
4. E-mail all volunteers within a certain time frame whether currently active or not.
5. Mail merge to print labels for volunteers who do not have e-mail.
6. Link to system-wide celebration efforts.
7. Use address info on invitations for events.

Recruiting

1. Application goes to designated staff person with backup options in case of staff absence.
2. Opportunities posted on http://www.kcls.org/volunteer.
3. Automated reminders of when postings expire.
4. Stats: number of inquiries, conversions to active volunteers.
5. Reports of who inquired, applied.
6. Customizable application for each program.
7. Staff access—what we can see, who can see it; what we can do; who can do it.
8. Branches edit only their branches/cluster volunteers.
9. Be able to see from anywhere, log in from anywhere.
10. Branches see branch and cluster information and some system information.
11. One login per cluster and for Outreach, unless only one person can use the login at one time. Then will need to determine number of logins required.
12. One login per system coordinator (one each for Study Zone, NetMasters, Citizenship, Talk Required).

Volunteer Access

1. Enter time only at physical location, not remotely.
2. Receive personal messages when checking in for shift.

3. Use one designated (but not fully dedicated) computer in each location to sign in and out.
4. Volunteers able to update their own information

Support

1. Don't want branches to have to do tech support for the volunteers (i.e., I can't get into the system, home computer not configured, etc.)
2. Volunteer Services Coordinator needs access to tech support (24/7?). Weekends/evenings?
3. Tech support coordinated through Central Volunteer Services Coordinator.
4. Backup ideas for if system is down.
5. Branch level tech support is not needed.

Data Conversion

1. Study Zone Access database.
2. Library volunteers Excel database.
3. Outreach Access database.
4. Talk Time/Citizenship MS Access databases.

Training

1. Volunteer training—want simple, simple, simple.
2. Staff training options: class for 1–2 representatives, then peer training.
3. Online tutorials.

CHOOSING THE INFORMATION YOU NEED:
WHAT KCLS CHOSE TO USE

Compare items in that long list with the data that KCLS actually collects and uses. Here is a summary of the data that currently is collected and used to communicate with and about volunteers.[8]

Basic numbers, by library/program and totaled:

Number of volunteers with hours recorded (these are considered the active volunteers).

Number of hours recorded

Outputs (by Library):

Study Zone: Number of sessions/total sessions, duration for each session/total duration, number of students in attendance/total attendance.

Talk Time: Number of sessions/total sessions, duration for each session/total duration, number of students in attendance/total attendance.

TechTutors: Number of sessions/total sessions, duration for each session/total duration, number of students in attendance/total attendance.

Citizenship: Number of sessions/total sessions, duration for each session/total duration, number of students in attendance/total attendance; plus number of students who come back to report that they passed the U.S. Naturalization Test.

Outreach: Number of volunteers and number of hours recorded.

Other miscellaneous information that we ask volunteers to record and can access when requested is:

Grades and subjects taught in Study Zone
One to One assistance sessions in TechTutors
Class subject taught by TechTutors
Number of students taught by TechTutors, by class subject
Hours needed for community service; name of school district or court
Employers that match employee volunteer hours with donations
Age ranges of volunteers

NONCOMMERCIAL RECORD-KEEPING CHOICES

Some libraries have a small enough volunteer pool that a commercial information system or local software development may not seem justified. Even with a small number of volunteers, however, it is important to have an efficient and complete way to keep track of who is volunteering, scheduling, and hours worked. Most librarians can use various electronic products to keep volunteer information in order. But you would need to create several products—an Excel spreadsheet to collect hours worked, a calendar to schedule volunteers, and a directory to keep volunteer contact information. None of these products are difficult to use, but data would likely need to be collected on paper and entered manually into your various documents.

Likewise, all volunteer records can be collected on paper. Volunteers and staff then need to be given uniform instructions on what information is needed, and where the forms are kept. Then staff need to keep track of the forms and compile data on a regular basis. Simple solutions are effective only if the data are collected and compiled consistently. Electronic compilation usually proves the easiest.

Perhaps most importantly, there is the issue of communication with volunteers in an increasingly electronic world. Not having even a simple volunteer management information system means that small libraries will be left with the job of constructing or changing e-mail or other electronic macros when it would be so much easier to set up a simple electronic system once and then make minor changes as needed but still with the potential advantage of wide distribution through the designated community receiving a particular communication.

CONCLUSION

To reiterate, take the list of data entry ideas that King County used as it set out to reform its volunteer program, decide what you need and don't need in this kind of a system, look at the systems that you can create, and purchase or rent from your automation vendor and/or from other organizational and commercial system vendors as well. Treat the project as a good way to review all the elements of your new or improved volunteer program. Your library will be the winner in many ways.

NOTES

1. *Volunteer Management Information System Army Volunteer Corps Volunteer User Guide* (Fort Sam Houston, TX: U.S. Army Family and MWR Command, June 2011), http://www.myarmyonesource.com/cmsresources/Army%20OneSource/Media/images/Family%20Programs%20and%20Services/Volunteering/VMIS_AVC_Volunteer_User_Guide.pdf (accessed April 7, 2013).

2. Volgistics is at http://www.capterra.com/sem/volunteer-management-software?gclid=CJyB8NmiubYCFQpxQgodHUEAKQ.

3. The Volgistics Libraries web page, http://www.volgistics.com/libraries.htm (accessed April 7, 2013).

4. VolunteerHub. *Managing Library Volunteers*, http://www.volunteerhub.com/clients/library-volunteers/ (accessed May 13, 2013).

5. CERVIS website, http://www.cervistech.com/ (accessed April 7, 2013).

6. The roadmap is at http://www.capterra.com/how-to-buy-software (accessed July 7, 2013).

7. "Volunteer, Define, Align, Empower: Developing a Coordinated Volunteer Program," Supporting Materials for KCLS Presentation at American Library Association Annual Conference, June 2011, New Orleans, LA Issaquah, WA: King County Library System, June 2011, 38–40.

8. Maria Hatcher and Terry Claypool to Glen Holt, e-mail communication, May 30, 2013, in author's possession.

9

The Future of Library Volunteerism

DIFFERENT FUTURES: LIBRARIANS, LIBRARIES, AND VOLUNTEERS

This book has been about three subjects: libraries, librarians, and volunteers. This chapter moves from description to modest foretelling, with emphasis on librarians and volunteers.

A pair of volunteerism experts, Susan J. Ellis and Katherine H. Campbell, authors of *By the People: A History of Americans as Volunteers*,[1] foretell the future of volunteerism. They write, "It seems safe to predict that the causes served by American volunteers will continue to change; the presence and commitment of volunteers will not."[2] Paraphrasing this thought for the topics of this book, as libraries and librarians change, so will the nature and the activities of library volunteers.

The future of libraries and librarianship is more nuanced, however. One of librarianship's notable futurists, David Lankes, author of *The Atlas of New Librarianship* (2011),[3] in a recent interview notes, "The future is going to be fewer libraries and more librarians. The facility is transitioning from places where librarians do their work to places where communities meet and gather."[4] Within this context, Lankes says, librarians can sit in any number of physical spaces, while "the electronic medium is where they can research and write." In other words, library facilities will evolve: some new ones will be built, and some will be rehabbed, while many will close.

Most readers know of libraries that have closed due to lack of support for their high operational costs or when those who funded them discerned that they met no public need. Closings and reductions in service can be followed on the *Huffington Post* "Libraries in Crisis" website at http://www.huffingtonpost.com/news/libraries-in-crisis/.

Other libraries have evolved. The recently opened Mansueto Library at the University of Chicago hosts a huge computer facility under its grand glass dome,[5] with books placed below; while the state of Minnesota moved most of its books and archives into the Elmer L. Anderson research library, with its two huge manmade caverns with their 1.5 million items that support pleasant research and reading rooms in the library's above-ground reading rooms.[6] Both Minnesota and Chicago use mechanized shelving and retrieval systems to fulfill user requests for books.

The Medical Library at Washington University in St. Louis left the book stacks in its old building and added a seven-story hardwired tower with some computers, but many positions where students can plug in their own gadgets to both electrical and high-speed Internet capabilities.[7] Anyone who walks through the new Medical Library tower at Washington University will find meeting rooms and classrooms of every size, including a conference room on the facility's top floor along with its rare books facility. All are equipped for graphic presentations and community conversations, including fund-raising conversations.

Charlotte Mecklenburg Library combined its main children's facility with the local children's theater to create Imaginon, which sets a new standard for the future of librarian and library services to youth.[8] It is a child-, family-, and teen-friendly place with three theaters (with set, costume, and sound/lighting support). Teens have their own space and there is an animation lab where kids can design their own films and games. And—oh, yes—there are books and computers for children preschool through high school.

The library at Minneapolis' Benilde–St. Margaret's High School has no books. The teachers took what they wanted of the print collection for use in the classroom and sent the rest of the 5,000-book collection to Africa. At the new, digital Benilde library, students can do research through online databases such as Gale and ProQuest and get help from math and literacy coaches. "We used to think of a library as a building with stacks of books," high school principal Sue Skinner told the *School Library Journal*. "Now we should think of it as a space where people come together to share ideas, be creative, access information, and even read. Instead of thinking of it so literally, we should think of it as a more active space and evolving."[9]

Each of these new library configurations was done to change how people use libraries, so volunteer jobs will change also. In computer-based libraries, a lot more volunteers will help train, tutor, and troubleshoot the user/computer interface. Oddly, volunteers may also spend more time with the print collection, as librarian time may be better spent with electronic resources that often require complex search protocols. While these libraries may develop all-new volunteer jobs, it is more likely that volunteer jobs will evolve as the library services change.

Lankes's more important prognostication about librarians involves a huge change in their work. Far less of their effort—even none in many cases—will involve books or artifacts. Rather, librarians' work will become the improvement of their current and potential user communities through knowledge creation. To put a finer point on the prediction, Lankes sees librarians becoming "facilitators of conversation" who interact with their communities to support their informational and learning needs.[10] Mastery of new technology will be assumed among future librarians; their work tasks will be "to enrich, capture, store and disseminate the conversations of their communities."

Lankes's *The Atlas of New Librarianship* is a fascinating read. It also is a tool—a map for the professional conversations that will be necessary to change librarians' work as they undertake new community-building activity. In social science terms, that role sounds more like a community organizer than a librarian. If that is to be the future, then the professional education of librarianship must change, with research, communication, outreach, and extension methods all receiving higher priority than they have presently in LIS education. If Lankes is right, all kinds of children's and adult services would appear to be on the increase as this redefinition of library work comes to the fore. Undoubtedly, too, there will be volunteers, including those from community organizations who will be involved in helping start conversations about reading and information needs and to help libraries capitalize on what is being said by users and potential users.

As the remainder of this chapter points out, volunteers are to be found playing myriad roles in the evolving library of the future. That's because volunteers are frequently involved in changes both large and small. And, that's because practitioner librarians use volunteers to assist in service or organizational innovations, as in, "Let's volunteer to do this" or "We'll use volunteers for that."

There is foreshadowing of the future in earlier chapters of this book. All of the examples in Chapter 2, those about library starting, funding, and advocating, and the big innovations in Chapter 3, like the Internet Public Library and using volunteers to further community literacy and computer literacy, are examples of how volunteers are playing roles in activities that help bring about a bright future for libraries. So, too, are examples from the Appendix, which lays out the thoughtful planning and the spirit of innovation that went into rehabilitating and reforming King County Public Library's volunteer program. You have found other examples in other chapters as well.

It is a cliché to say that the adaptation of professional librarians is a foundation of the profession. But the cliché is true. Few librarians would disagree with legendary futurist and science fiction guru Isaac Asimov when he wrote, "The only constant is change, continuing change, inevitable change; that is the dominant factor in society today. No sensible decision can be made any longer without taking into account not only the world as it is, but the world as it will be."[11] That ability to adapt, however, does not make change easy, especially when it affects individuals in an unpredictable and personalized way. Richard "Dick" Marcinko, the first commanding officer of U.S. Navy SEAL Team Six who is now a motivational speaker, writes about this impact: "Change hurts. It makes people insecure, confused, and angry. People want things to be the same as they've always been, because that makes life easier. But, if you're a leader, you can't let your people hang on to the past."[12]

Many librarians and volunteers see the changes in the library the way Marcinko describes them. It has come abruptly and in grainy snapshots or out-of-focus movies. Only in hindsight do library changes seem neat and tidy. This contrast can be seen in the artistic renderings of the probable early-day Library of Alexander in Kelly Trimble's 2003 "children's book" describing that institution[13] or in the orderly architectural photographs of the University of Alexander's *Bibliotheca Alexandrina* on the web.[14] The character of real library change is seen in the end of "library writing," which removed a whole category of specialized work from professional librarianship; in distinctive old Carnegie library buildings transformed into "cute" restaurants or residences; and in the messy birth of the discipline of information science, which has wended its way out of library science, computer science, and education through many recent decades. Change is messy. And hardly any change that involves knowledge creation is clear—except in hindsight.

LIBRARIANS USE VOLUNTEERS AS AN ADAPTATION MECHANISM

When change—especially large change—has occurred in the United States, volunteers have appeared more quickly than National Guard troops after a disaster. Like all professionals, librarians face their most difficult adjustment time when some change radically affects the way they work. Librarianship began as an ordering of the knowledge universe both by figuring out how to shelve books (i.e., discrete containers of information and data) and to create relatively clear pathways into paper-based knowledge within books and journals. Like the population generally, some librarians have quickly adopted the new "metadata" methodologies, but RDA (Resource Description and Access) is now shifting the granularity of what can be described. Volunteers have worked beside librarians to achieve new kinds of information sorting and characterization. Some of these referents (for example, senior citizens) are available to answer questions on Skype, Facebook, and Twitter either through the library website or on other online locations.[15] Most are operated by individuals or groups of citizens who volunteer their time and share their special knowledge without cost.

VOLUNTEERS AS INFORMATION PROVIDERS

The reaction of library professionals to technology changes have been mostly to declare them a good thing and—as money permitted—to hasten their inclusion among the up-to-date libraries with computer catalogs and electronic databases all hooked up to the Internet. The "personal device revolution" is still early in its cycle, and while some libraries have started this transition, others are still trying to sort out how the new personalized technology will impact their constituents.

In the meantime, volunteers have started their own websites where potential library users can find them. All volunteer information sites are part of the electronic competition for libraries that operate in a single place. They serve to point out that a library filled with "reference professionals" may or may not be able to provide answers to information seekers that is as good as websites operated by all kinds of volunteer professionals in addition to those willing to do many kinds of activities as a fee-based service.

One such group is the Elder Wisdom Circle. Their website opens with these words: "Need advice on your family, relationship, self-improvement and career questions? Not sure where to turn? This is the place where people in their teens, 20s, 30s, and beyond connect with Cyber-Grandparents for confidential, personal, and compassionate guidance."[16] This site is staffed completely by volunteers.[17] No medical, legal, or financial advice is offered. It is a wonderful example of how anonymous, specialized Internet communities are developing. Nothing is changing faster in libraries than the nature of reference and research questions. And, the nature of the Elder Wisdom Circle is that volunteers are serving as reference "experts" to answer the public's questions.

Another example comes on the free information page of the King County (Washington) Bar Association, entitled "Legal Advice. We May Be Able to Help." The bar association volunteers offer individual and group legal advice on consumer issues, estate planning, family law, public benefits, general legal advice, housing, and dealing with criminal records. The site also has information on how poor persons can get individual pro-bono services from an attorney who is a member of the association. All attorneys who give free help are practicing professionals who are members of the bar association.[18] They give help as volunteers.

The Mayo Clinic has an excellent reference site offering medical information. The popular medical information available from the National Library of Medicine's Medline probably is the best known. The Mayo Clinic's Find It Fast offers a self-help selection process that can take you from a list of symptoms to a set of questions you should ask a specialist medical person about.[19] One can argue that Mayo's experts are not volunteers, but in the minds of individuals searching for medical information, it is a free offering of readable and visual information that helps persons communicate with medical professionals.

Free genealogy and free local history sites are just as numerous as free medical and legal sites, but without professional standards plus ethical and legal requirements that are built into the fabric of these two professions, these sites are highly variable in what they propose to do for those who visit them. It is enough to say that each of these specialties has a profusion of advisees, many of whom are volunteers. It has been great fun for this book's authors to find sites that provide enormous amounts of free information about family members, often presenting wholly new insights into their lives. A great deal of this information, of course, is from volunteers who are showing off their work even as they seek obscure pieces of information about their own relatives.

A business assistance site has some of the same mixed motives. Operating under the tagline "Make our Experience Your Success," Business Mentors New Zealand has over 1,600 experienced business professionals who will help out start-ups and troubled smaller businesses make the shift to successful operations. One of Business Mentors New Zealand's partner-sponsors is Statistics New Zealand, which offers "Market Mapper" and "Business Profiler" so that prospecting businesses can get a bead on both the market they want to capture and the shape of the competition they face. The mentors program also helps out the Pacific Business Mentoring Programme, which provides assistance to businesses in other Pacific Island nations.[20]

There is the issue that individuals have to "go to the library" either through their own effort or by using some mechanical or technological device, all of which have a time cost built into them. Some prospective users may decide that it is easier to use volunteers on the Internet than to make the effort to go to the library and seek out "the right librarian" to find out some piece of information.[21] Such a possibility does not create the need for breast beating about how good libraries are, but sustained efforts to make as many libraries as possible into quality-oriented, essential institutions that meet specific needs of their constituents in multiple accessible ways.

WHERE VOLUNTEERS FIT IN CHANGING LIBRARIES

So, do libraries embrace these volunteer information sources, or do they ignore them? Do libraries acknowledge the value of these sites and recommend them to library users? Do they recruit these same volunteer information specialists to come volunteer at the library/?

Through the twentieth century, volunteers came in waves to help American libraries hard hit by two world wars, a worldwide depression, and a population that grew by leaps and bounds. However, in the United States right now, there are more persons seeking places as volunteers than in any previous generation. Many want to help libraries handle the onslaught as entertainment and education become more popular and more prolific. As knowledge and professional library tasks expand, volunteer assignments grow more numerous. And, many libraries experience the uncomfortable pressure of having more volunteers who want positions than the institutions have the capability of training and supervising them.

Throughout this book you have seen multiple illustrations of where volunteers fit into many different types of libraries. Many of those illustrations show how libraries have used volunteers to help deal with their staffing problems and to introduce service reorganizations as well. Volunteers became a dynamic supplement to accomplish library work tasks that needed to be done.

So, if volunteers have played and continue to play so many important roles in libraries, where's the problem? Acknowledging that as libraries vary so do volunteer programs, and that there is no one model volunteer program that will fit in every library, why does the coming or reforming of volunteers in any library seem so difficult? Why does a sensible American tradition of volunteers rooted in antebellum America make some librarians uncomfortable when some reform involving them is suggested in a twenty-first-century library?

The fundamental answer is fear of competition and loss of control over one's own job and perhaps one's salary as well. In short, the introduction and use of volunteers too often is seen as a management-labor issue rather than a way of helping a successful library improve its services and products. Erica A. Nicol and Corey M. Johnson in a 2008 article argue that the most powerful reason to support volunteer programs is that they provide resources that enable libraries to move toward a "consultation model of communication." The authors' enthusiasm comes from their seeing the opportunity to break down "the 'fast-food' system of customer service." For them, that means breaking the "temporal and functional" limits of how librarians "help" patrons. Volunteers allow librarians to move to a "consultation model" involving "in-depth discussion of the patron's needs." Facilitating problem solving is a far better paradigm, implying more direct involvement in the process of under-standing that occurs in users.[22]

UNCERTAIN VOLUNTEER USE

Some librarians embrace volunteerism, and others appear to be uncertain about how to deal with volunteerism in their organizations. For example, if you insert a Google search for "Widener Library, Harvard, volunteer opportunities" or a similar word-search string, you pull up the names and vita of a few Widener staff who volunteer at some other library in metro Boston and a few divisions that apparently use volunteers, but you'll be hard-pressed to find an extensive amount of volunteer activity acclaimed among the many achievements of this great university research library. The same thing occurs in a similar search for Yale University Library volunteers. Neither of these two libraries is known to hold any of its lights under a bushel. If either of these institutions has a robust volunteer program, why aren't they bragging about it?

On the West Coast, the University of California, Berkeley library proudly announces its volunteer participation and recruitment. There is a caveat, however; that is currency. The electronic advertisement reads, "The UC Berkeley Library Volunteer Program is a pilot program, consisting of a group of library enthusiasts who generously contribute their time and talents to the Library."[23] Library jobs are posted on *Volunteer Match*, in the prescribed application process.[24] The posting from March 2010 suggests volunteering is new, not an established tradition at Berkeley, which is in so many other ways is a bastion of free expression. If it has been changed, the web announcement has not.

The Library of Congress lumps volunteer opportunities with work-study and internships. The slight but ringing endorsement of one group of LC volunteers is described as follows: "This volunteer activity offers the individual the opportunity to serve at our five busy Information Desks, in the Jefferson and Madison Buildings."[25] The contact of most professional librarians with volunteers, however, appears minimal at best.

If you actually like library volunteer programs and think they are important, you get more warm feelings about this subject when you look up New York Public Library (NYPL) than you do when perusing many large academic libraries. NYPL uses the web as a huge recruitment site, calling for volunteers at more than a dozen of its branches, including the research center on 42nd Street. NYPL wants Spanish speakers, help organizing romance novels and movies, workers with teens, those with tech sense sufficient to repair and ready digital and audio machinery in the Braille and Talking Book Library, computer helpers, docents to give tours, and information desk clerks in the 42nd Street Research Library. In short, NYPL will take free help when it needs it to do many different tasks at several different branches.

From NYPL's quite typical listing, however, there is one announcement unusual by public library standards because it steps over the "Everybody's doin' it" line to suggest how volunteers can help the institution's future users. Its web page calls for online volunteers who will "collaborate with NYPL to build the library of the future! We're doing this with the help of volunteers. **We're exploring new and fun ways of improving access to rare and unique collections online**. These are projects you can work on anytime, anywhere with an internet connection. We have two active initiatives now. More are on the way!" (emphasis added).[26] What smart computer user who secretly thinks he knows more than librarians about some subject could resist this plea for virtual volunteer recruits?

The Indiana State Library (ISL) knows the same secret about volunteers as NYPL.[27] ISL calls for volunteers to help in unwrapping, photographing, and documenting an extensive Indiana art collection and several positions in the Indiana Talking Books and Braille Library recording books and magazines published in and about Indiana and not otherwise available electronically. As with NYPL and Berkeley, the work for the Talking Books and Braille Library can be accomplished on site or virtually.

EMERGING ISSUES

An intriguing statement about the future of libraries—and with that, possible inferences about the future of library volunteer work—comes from Brisbane, Australia, where in 2006, the Brisbane City Council sponsored a meeting to discuss the future of libraries. "Representatives included directors of the Brisbane City Council library, head of facilities, social planners as well as representatives of the community, for example, publishers, website designers, architects, futurists, directors of policy think tanks and academics." The question for discussion: "Are libraries conceptualizing their future?"[28]

The meeting leaders began by proposing a set of "Provocative Discussion Points." These points concerned the present and future of government, of libraries, and of the people who worked in these institutions. Accepting these "discussion points" (i.e., "emerging issues") as elements of future libraries, what is their implication for the future of volunteers? What follows are issues for all libraries to consider inspired by the Brisbane agenda.

Libraries Face Decreasing Funding and Higher Costs

In this situation, if libraries are to remain open, user fees will increase, and specialty libraries will appear. Great Britain has just gone through a decade-long funding cutback, insisting on each library earning more of its operating income, cutting its book budgets, and depending much more heavily on computer catalogs and databases. Medical school libraries, municipal reference libraries, court and related law libraries, and school libraries have experienced similar reduced funding. Volunteers have been part of the solution to budget cutbacks throughout U.S. library history; in the short and/or long term, volunteers can be expected to be part of the change equation. The same thing can be said of international demand for librarians. Canadian students training to become professional librarians set up a group they call "Librarians without Borders." Students from that group already have discovered that their talents are wanted internationally.[29]

Education and Experience for Successful Librarianship Will Become More Specialized

Even more than it has been in the past, "general reference" will become the intersection of a multiple-direction traffic stop, not in itself a place where everyone comes to get answers. Librarians who write books and articles already have taken this change into account, writing about the new roles that librarians play under the new conditions. The preferred present and future model has been the "information consultant," someone who helps virtual and in-person users find data and information wherever it can be found, whether organized databases, esoteric websites, or individuals. Volunteers will be trained to conduct a reference interview with library users to give directional and ready reference, while librarians are free to provide the more in-depth information specialist service. As described earlier in this chapter, volunteers already are involved in this aspect of the library present and future.

Libraries Offer Experiences in the Library

Libraries offer instruction in particular skill sets, like makers spaces, community engagement, content creation, or job skills such as those found in schools, universities and communities throughout the United States. "Librarians will focus on community engagement, content creation and use of emerging technologies. Libraries become places for incubating community innovation, co-creation and engagement in culture and knowledge. ... Library buildings as examples of 'green' and even developing cradle to grave green technologies for books and for facilities design."[30] Volunteers with cultural, civic, and environmental knowledge will help the library provide meaningful community (or school or university) experiences.

The Library as a Place for Escape from a Chaotic World

Many library users want to hold the library responsible for slowing time. "As the world quickens and moves to hyper-time and culture, libraries find desirable user niches by providing places of quietness and calm."[31] Volunteers will welcome library visitors and help librarians monitor quiet areas.

Digitization Offers another Challenge

The future possibility is for the librarian to become the "digital avatar, interacting with users, learning about their changing needs, and even in the longer term, organizing our memories."[32] That kind of future goes beside the death of the print book and the emergence of new 3-D and multiple-sense participatory stories. Those who contemplate such a work role will have to deal with the consuming isolation that for at least some users is part of participation in electronic community life. Virtual volunteers will have an increasing role in e-library services.

THE FUTURE OF LIBRARY VOLUNTEERISM

And, within this context of vastly changing institution, what do we expect to be the future of volunteers in libraries? Volunteerism has gained and shed many nuances since its inception as a concept around 1600. Australian academic Sohail Inayatullah writes: "Historically, volunteerism was central to society, it was part of community building, tak[ing] ... care of others, indeed, central to agricultural/

feudal society. It was especially strong in religious systems."[33] As societal constraints change, so too will volunteerism.

For example, if the need for paid work shifted, the market for volunteers would change as well. One suggestion is that "only 10 percent of the future US population will work for money. That suggests that 90% may become volunteers."[34] In that scenario, the question is not if they will volunteer, but whether or not potential volunteers will represent a permanent and ill-educated underclass seeking to find perhaps hidden ways into the paid workforce or if they are economically comfortable beings seeking intellectual or spiritual sustenance in a culture dominated by few receiving monetary rewards.[35] It is this kind of vision that helps fuel resistance to volunteerism in any organization, including libraries.

The growth of virtual volunteerism is one important change that will affect libraries in the next several decades, with all the shifts in communication, definition, and supervision that such a change implies. Virtual volunteering will certainly grow, because in a time of information abundance, the respected specialization will not be for how many books are held, but how much data, information, and knowledge is made easily accessible. And, even if many librarians hold volunteerism in ambivalence, that does not mean that some institutions will not find mechanisms to fit both on-site and virtual volunteering into their production forces.

Here are ten ways that we will see library volunteerism evolve in the future.

Virtual Volunteerism

The biggest *Present Shock* change for libraries, one that author Douglas Rushkoff suggests has just started, is to deal constructively with the virtual world.[36] In the future, libraries, like all other businesses, will be increasingly virtual; that is, their services will be assembled and their products and services requested and delivered online. In that setting, the opportunities for volunteers will be enhanced.[37] Tessa Spencer offers a good summary of how to build a virtual volunteer community—for a nature-based organization. The tenets of this success are conversation and collaboration, exactly those that Lankes puts forth in his book on the future of libraries.[38]

The growth of virtual volunteerism, discussed in the previous section, is one important change that will affect libraries in the next several decades, with all the shifts in communication, definition, and supervision that such a change implies. Virtual volunteering will certainly grow, because in a time of information abundance, the respected specialization will be not for how many books are held, but for how much data, information, and knowledge is made easily accessible. Even if many librarians hold volunteerism in ambivalence, that does not mean that some institutions will not find mechanisms to fit both on-site and virtual volunteering into their production forces. And, the economics of these individuals and sites will be based differently from most libraries with their old-fashioned industrial bureaucracies.

Here is a summary of advantages for virtual volunteering from Serviceleader .org.

- Volunteer managers can use online discussion groups via e-mail or live chat as a centerpiece of interaction.

- "New groups of volunteers are emerging," and virtual volunteering is a good way to recruit new persons and turn them into "long-term supporters, even donors."
- Virtual volunteers may have better computer equipment and software and more sophisticated skill sets than on your staff.[39]

The trend toward more virtual volunteering will be tied up with the future of social media. Jackie Norris, senior adviser to the Corporation for National and Community Service since 2009, says, "Social media is going to be the driver of volunteerism in the future. ... Social media will be the hub [that brings] more people together, and you'll also see more fund raising and greater potential for volunteering. ... Technology is going to broaden volunteerism."[40]

Virtual volunteering, of course, has the same planning sequence as on-site volunteering. To think about the impact of the increase in virtual competition, analyze how work currently gets done and how current work in a unit might be made virtual.[41] What would your library do if only 15 percent of its whole business was on-site, within a library's physical spaces? What would it grow? What would it eliminate? The opportunities for virtual volunteering are endless for libraries, and the benefits of this change look good as well.[42]

Another kind of help for analyzing virtual volunteering can be inferred from taking a look at the task list in *Successful Management in the Virtual Office* (1995) by Bruce McGraw and Bernie Kelly. As old as this book is, virtual volunteering jobs already included:

- Answering user or staff questions
- Cataloging/tagging, indexing, abstracting
- Data entry, data processing, data analysis
- Programming, maintaining databases
- Project-oriented work/management (arranging for speakers, marketing, etc.)
- Recordkeeping
- Research
- Sending/receiving e-mail
- Spreadsheet analysis
- Word processing
- Writing

Modern librarians would be hard-pressed to claim that any of these tasks required paid employees to sit at desks in a single building to get them accomplished.

Short-Term Volunteerism Will Continue to Grow to Match Rising Short-Term Employment

The nature of employment is changing from lengthy employment with one company or government agency to many more persons putting together short-term jobs, holding two or three jobs together to earn a living and more volunteering to gain experience in order to gain training for a new for a job. There also will be more short-term volunteers. That means that librarians who need people to ramp up on a job assignment but who for one reason or another can't hire those persons will have to connect short-term volunteer assignments to get the work done and to have impact on the institution's services and the community. In such situations, searches tend to be extended, as organizations seek optimal candidates. The whole employment scene will have more employment flux than in recent past decades. This point is documented earlier in this book.

More Pressure to Create Internships—i.e., More Formal Job Training

There will be more pressure on schools, legislative bodies, courts, and even prisons to create more internships, more school-credit work-study, and more court-ordered services. Economics and job-training needs to prepare for employment will drive this set of relationships. This item is another way of saying that the public will expect a little money to go a long way. So, there will be pressure on libraries to sponsor paid or supervise paid and unpaid internships to teach certain computer-related job skills to potential new employees. Because so much court-ordered work involves assignment to heavy labor, libraries will be pushed to take on more interns and court-ordered assignees in order to help train workers for other jobs. In other words, librarians will be pressured to organize more training options. When other formal educational institutions seem to be unable to do the job, pressure grows on legatee educational institutions like libraries to pick up educational pieces.

Pressure on Libraries to Export Their Job Training Away from Their Buildings

Libraries might begin to export some of their volunteer job training from their own institutions to classrooms, the student union, senior centers, homeless shelters, and community groups. If a library has a highly visible volunteer program that is known for its useful training, its community leaders might be expected to ask that such training would occur outside the library. To sum up this point, as libraries develop their reputation as volunteer trainers, it is not unthinkable that they would be asked to train in other community institutions either on a for-hire basis or for some form of beneficial cooperation from a prospective partner. To finish this point, remember that library volunteerism never occurs in isolation. As a high-visibility organization, when schools, employers, and other government agencies are facing trouble, there will likely be pressure to shift libraries into educational and experience-giving institutions, training offsite as well as on-site.

Volunteer Managers Will Get More Professional, and Certification Will Increase

This trend began in the 1980s under the leadership of the Association for Volunteer Administration.[43] The related work of the Council for Certification of Volunteer Administration adds pressure to produce a set quality of leadership competencies to operate a volunteer program. Moreover, many states, universities, and even some larger communities are finding ways to certify volunteer leaders.

Volunteers Will Be Pressed into Service as Volunteer Trainers

As changes occur in technology, the economy, education, community demographics, and attitudes about the role of volunteerism—and if we assume that volunteer management certification will increase—then won't there be new demands for training and task mentoring for those performing volunteer labor? As volunteerism in libraries grows through time, effort and investment will be needed to train volunteers.

More Specialized Jobs Will Be Done by Volunteers

General reference and collection development are done by staff, but sophisticated specialties such as archives, genealogy or maps will be done by volunteers. An intriguing example comes from a publication by a library staff member who used graduate librarian interns from distant schools, training them in the issues of international librarianship to prepare materials for the University of Houston Digital Library as well as the South Asian American Digital Archive.[44]

Volunteer Cadres Will Be Formed around Information Consultant Librarians

What is the future of the professional librarian as an information consultant? Purportedly in this model of librarianship, the librarian collects information from multiple sources both inside a specific library and virtually from whatever sources are available electronically. As this consulting becomes the norm, this person would need volunteers to do research, aggregate materials, and create materials lists to support the staff information consultant. In other words, the information/consultant librarian would hold metadata projects together. These volunteers would need to have search skills and subject knowledge, but they would not need to work in the library or even be in the same geographic region as the library. Instead, "computer-pal model librarians" could recruit volunteers from around the world who contribute and benefit from the exchange of information in a specific library's work group.

When More Libraries Close, Volunteers Will Move to Operate Many of Them

There is a near ironclad law in the United States that when library systems, schools, or universities close libraries or even threaten to close libraries, a group of citizens, parents, students, or professors steps forward to maintain or open a library, or to build a new library to replace the old one, on a volunteer basis. That is especially true if the service area or its population is not without financial and time resources. Tight economic times will only add to the pressure to move things along the all-volunteer path. All-volunteer libraries or "almost-all volunteer libraries" may well become the norm in service to some user communities.

Volunteerism Is a Way That Libraries Can Add Value to Their Measured Outcomes

There is a federal law, the Government Performance and Results Act (GPRA) passed in 1993, that says that any library that takes federal money has to be able to measure the outcomes of its effort.[45] To keep up with that law, volunteerism will certainly become part of the calculation of outcome benefits. Libraries will develop outcomes or positive impacts of library volunteers and report them as library impacts or outcomes. It will be very surprising if libraries do not get more caught up in externally driven formula calculations to demonstrate their benefits to direct users and to society generally. In such instances, volunteerism would seem to be a very significant element to add to a library's benefits equation.

A CONCLUDING WORD ABOUT LIBRARY VOLUNTEERISM

To conclude, consider how we began this book: "Everybody's doin' it. Everybody's doin' volunteers." Within that broad observation, what should libraries do about volunteerism?

Volunteerism is a traditional American tool that library professionals can use wisely to improve the quality of their literacy and information future. To put the conclusion into a policy question: Within economic, social, and legal constraints, how should librarians use volunteers to improve the quality of constituent services even as they advance their own institutional cause? The answers will not all be the same. But, as shown in this book, there are many good answers for many different libraries. Finding the right answers for your library is a win-win situation. A well-managed volunteer program will undoubtedly add value to your library and benefit your volunteers.

NOTES

1. Susan J. Ellis and Katherine H. Campbell, *By the People: A History of Americans as Volunteers* (Philadelphia: Energize, Century Edition, 2005).

2. Susan J. Ellis and Katherine H. Campbell, "Volunteering: An American Tradition," posted December 30, 2011, http://iipdigital.usembassy.gov/st/english/publication/2011/11/20111114165203nasus0.1764032.html#ixzz2YC4j8vho (accessed July 5, 2013).

3. David Lankes, *The Atlas of New Librarianship* (Cambridge, MA: MIT Press, 2011).

4. World Future Society, "The Futurist Interviews Librarian Futurist David Lankes," http://www.wfs.org/content/futurist-interviews-librarian-futurist-david-lankes (accessed July 4, 2013).

5. Photos and description available at http://mansueto.lib.uchicago.edu/ (accessed July 7, 2013).

6. Illustrations, photos and description available at https://www.lib.umn.edu/special/about-andersen-library (accessed July 7, 2013).

7. Washington University's Becker Medical Library building and service are described at https://becker.wustl.edu/ (accessed July 7, 2013).

8. Imaginon is described at http://www.imaginon.org/ (accessed July 7, 2013).

9. Huffington Post Libraries in Crisis website, "Minneapolis School Library without Books Thrives after Clearing Entire Print Collection," http://www.huffingtonpost.com/2013/01/09/minneapolis-schools-libra_n_2442171.html?utm_hp_ref=libraries-in-crisis (accessed July 7, 2013).

10. World Future Society, "Futurist Interviews."

11. http://www.thephoenixprinciple.com/quotes/2004/11/isaac_asimov_th.html (accessed June 16, 2009).

12. ThinkExist.com, http://thinkexist.com/quotation/change-hurts-it-makes-people-insecure-confused/397083.html (accessed July 10, 2013).

13. Kelly Trimble, *The Library of Alexandria*, illus. Robina MacIntyre Marshall (New York: Houghton Mifflin, Clarion, 2003).

14. Wikipedia, "Bibliotheca Alexandrina," http://en.wikipedia.org/wiki/Bibliotheca_Alexandrina (accessed May 18, 2013). Or, examine the English guide to the library at http://www.bibalex.org/Home/Default_EN.aspx (accessed May 18, 2013).

15. Access to all three is available at *Seniors Internet Help*, http://seniorsinternethelp.com/ (accessed July 1, 2013), and there are many, many others.

16. Elder Wisdom Circle, http://www.elderwisdomcircle.org/ (accessed May 18, 2013).

17. In 2005, this site was named the Internet Personal Advice Community of Seniors. We published an announcement about it in "Learning Sites, References and Notes," *Public Library Quarterly* 24, no. 3 (2005), http://www.elderwisdomcircle.org/ (accessed July 13, 2005).

18. King County (WA) Bar Association, "Legal Issues? We May Be Able to Help," http://www.kcba.org/pbs/legalhelp.aspx (accessed April 10, 2013).

19. Mayo Clinic, "Find It Fast," http://www.mayoclinic.com/health-information/ (accessed April 10, 2013).

20. Ray Schofield, "Helping Business Owners Out of Sticky Situations," *NZ Business* 24, no. 11 (December 2010): 68. Also, *Business Mentors New Zealand*, http://businessmentors.org.nz/ and http://www.stats.govt.nz/ (accessed April 12, 2013).

21. Larry Nash White, *Competition for Library Services: For the Inspiration, Innovation, and Celebration Conference for Librarians*, June 18, 2009, http://www.slideshare.net/lockmb/competition-for-library-services (accessed April 10, 2013).

22. Erica A. Nicol and Corey M. Johnson, "Volunteers in Libraries: Program Structure, Evaluation, and Theoretical Analysis,"*Reference and User Services Quarterly* 48, no. 2 (2009): 154–63. See also Robert S. Taylor, "Question-Negotiation and Information Seeking in Libraries," *College and Research Libraries* 29 (May 1968): 178–94, which is the principal source used by the authors to substantiate this conclusion.

23. UC Berkeley Library, Human Resources, "Volunteering at the Library." http://www.lib.berkeley.edu/LHRD/volunteerprogram.html (accessed May 16, 2013).

24. UC Berkeley Library, Human Resources, "Prospective Volunteer Information," http://www.lib.berkeley.edu/LHRD/volunteer.html (accessed May 16, 2013).

25. Library of Congress, "Working at the Library," http://www.loc.gov/hr/employment/index.php?action=cFellowships.showHome (accessed May 16, 2013).

26. New York Public Library, "Volunteer at NYPL," http://www.nypl.org/help/about-nypl/volunteer-nypl (accessed May 15, 2013).

27. Indiana State Library, "Volunteer Opportunities," http://www.in.gov/library/2364.htm (accessed May 18, 2013).

28. Sohail Inayatullah, "Which Future for Libraries?" *Foresight* 9, no. 3(2007): 54–57, http://faculty.taylor.edu/dnbowell/seminar08/wf.pdf (accessed May 18, 2013).

29. See the articles about LWB students in South Africa, Guatemala, and South Africa, http://lwb-online.org/?cat=4 (accessed July 4, 2013).

30. Inayatullah, "Which Future for Libraries?" 55.

31. Ibid.

32. Ibid.

33. Sohail Inayatullah, "The Futures of Volunteerism," Metafuture.org, http://www.metafuture.org/Articles/The_Futures_of_Volunteerism.htm (accessed May 18, 2013).

34. Ibid.

35. Susan J. Ellis and Jayne Cravens, *The Virtual Volunteering Guidebook: How to Apply the Principles of Real-World Volunteer Management to Online Service* (Austin, TX: Impact Online, Inc. 2000). The virtual edition of this older volume is available free at http://www.service leader.org/sites/default/files/file/vvguide.pdf (accessed July 4, 2013).

36. Douglas Rushkoff, *Present Shock: When Everything Happens Now* (New York: Current Books, 2013).

37. Jane Cravens, "Telecommuting/Cloud Computing and Virtual Teams: Advocacy and Resources," revised April 13, 2013, http://www.coyotecommunications.com/work/telecommute.shtml (accessed September 3, 2013).

38. Tessa Spencer, "The Potential of the Internet for Non-Profit Organizations," *First Monday: Peer-Reviewed Journal on the Internet* 7, no. 8 (August 5, 2002), http://ojs-prod-lib .cc.uic.edu/ojs/index.php/fm/article/view/976/897 (accessed July 7, 2013).

39. Serviceleader.org, "Benefits of Virtual Volunteering," http://www.serviceleader.org/virtual/vvbenefits (accessed December 11, 2011).

40. Associations Now, "A Look at the Future of Volunteerism," interview by Samantha Whitehome, At http://www.asaecenter.org/Resources/ANowDetail.cfm?ItemNumber=51791 (accessed July 4, 2013).

41. Serviceleader.org, "Benefits of Virtual Volunteering."

42. Ibid.

43. http://www.cvacert.org/about.htm#background (accessed July 6, 2013).

44. R. Niccole Westbrook, "How to Use Free Online Tools to Recruit and Manage Remote LIS Interns," *Library Leadership and Management* 26, no. 3–4 (2012): 1–19.

45. A convenient summary of this legislation is in Glen E. Holt, "Exploring Public Library Contributions to Urban Resiliency," in *Public Libraries and Resilient Cities*, ed. Michael Dudley (Chicago: ALA, 2013), 43.

Appendix

A Success Model: Integrating a Volunteer Program into the King County Library

This Appendix presents a case study of how one large urban public library successfully reformed its volunteer program. The library that made this change, the King County (Washington) Library System, has received wide recognition for the breadth and quality of its operations, including its handling of volunteers. Local acclaim has come from all kinds of agencies acknowledging its programs and services. The principal honor within the profession came from *Library Journal*, which named KCLS the 2011 Library of the Year. And, ALA asked KCLS to conduct a seminar on how it had reformed its volunteer program at the 2011 New Orleans Convention.

KCLS offers a great model because its reform effort dealt with most of the issues that a library of any size—including those that are very small and special libraries as well—might face when starting a new volunteers program or making major changes in its continuing program.

KCLS has a long tradition of autonomy in its volunteer program development in both the branch and system-wide service units. KCLS also lends itself to our purposes because it has published many of the documents related to its volunteer reform efforts. Much of the material in this Appendix is drawn from or based on elements in the publication that KCLS issued to attendees at the 2011 ALA seminar held in New Orleans.[1]

Sections that are direct quotes from KCLS documents will be found in specially formatted sections. Our analytical commentary runs before and after the KCLS documents.

KCLS' ANALYSIS OF ITS VOLUNTEER PROBLEMS[2]

In 2008, KCLS began a complex, multiyear period of appraisal and organizational reform that brought, among other things, massive and positive changes to the way it recruited, selected, supervised, and honored its volunteers. To help with the process of this evaluation and reform, the KCLS effort boasted effective administrators and a library system that had solid funding. More than most any process of library volunteer reform researched for this book, this one was vetted by actual application to solving a wide range of issues. The library system already had several volunteer programs operating, but they operated as unconnected pieces that did not work with each other or for the system as a whole. Taken together, these features meant that the library had the ability to move through the steps of volunteer reform in a rigorous, comprehensive, and methodical way. As the library progressed in its endeavor, it documented the reforms and published a manual reiterating what KCLS staff and the library's leaders had learned and what other libraries could learn from its efforts.

Virtually any library, even medium-size and small libraries, can learn a great deal from KCLS reforms. Even the smallest of institutions is likely to have to cope with several of the issues that King County experienced. And, while lack of funding may slow a particular library's reform process, it should not be the reason for not appraising the organization's volunteer program as a whole with the view to how volunteers will enhance library public services.

DECISION TO SURVEY STAFF AND RESULTS

The KCLS administration took a collaborative approach in responding to staff concerns about the institution's volunteer programs. That collaborative stance is evidenced in the way that the library's Administrative Planning Team (APT) addressed issues raised by staff. Staff told APT that volunteer efforts were uneven, with users complaining that volunteer services and opportunities they found at one community library were not available at their own libraries or those of their friends and schoolmates. It appeared that the diversity in volunteer programs was causing problems in public and staff perceptions about what the library was doing here and not there, for others and not us, in one type of KCLS library and not another of the same type.

KCLS administrators decided that they needed systematic information before moving forward to plan a new volunteers program. They obtained that information with a survey of staff. In one form or another, every library should occasionally survey both volunteers and staff to see if the program is working, and to be sure that it is achieving the stated program goals and outcomes. A small school library could ask volunteers to fill out a short survey at the end of the year to check both that volunteers understood the volunteer program and that it was successful in their experience. A large academic volunteer program could ask volunteer leaders the same questions to have a quick and easy check of how the volunteer program was working.

The KCLS survey given to 200 staff members documented the difficulties of the volunteer programs already going on within the system. The survey confirmed the initial staff complaints: The volunteer program needed major attention if it was

Table A.1

Staff Information about Volunteers: Results of a KCLS Survey

Question	Agree	Disagree	Staff Comments
I have a clear under-standing of the role of the library's volunteers and the staff who supervise them.	48.7%	33.2%	"Our branch staff have worked (and continue to work together to clarify expectations and tasks and to specify staff roles." "It is unclear to me what exactly volunteers are allowed to do, what union rules prevent or restrict them from doing, etc. Why isn't it the same at every branch? We need more clarity and more consistency."
Current communication practices regarding li-brary volunteers and staff who supervise them are inadequate.	28%	35.4%	"There is no communication." "Without any clear direction, we often times worry that we may be utilizing our volunteers incorrectly."
The library's policies and guidelines for vo-lunteers and staff who supervise them are clear.	26.6%	29.4%	"What guidelines?" "It is inconsistent from branch to branch."
I receive support, ma-terials and training to successfully supervise library volunteers	9.2%	49.1%	"I think it should be more uniform than it is, consistent at all branches. ... We need volunteer manuals, training checklists, etc." "This is definitely an 'every man for himself' zone at our library."

Source: KCLS, "Volunteer, Define, Align, Empower: Developing a Coordinated Volunteer Program," Supporting Materials for KCLS Presentation at American Library Association Annual Conference June 2011, New Orleans, LA (Issaquah, WA: King County Library System, June 2011).

going to be made into a more significant part of KCLS operations. Table A.1 contains the tabulated results of that 2008 survey.

PLANNING CHANGES IN THE VOLUNTEER PROGRAM

The way that KCLS reformed its volunteer program demonstrates a clear progression that can be emulated by other library systems. In order to make the reforms of the volunteer program successful, four areas of library life needed improvement. These were the areas of:

1. Management
2. Staff communication
3. Recruitment
4. Training

Management

In writing the KCLS plan, the leaders "recommend[ed] consistent processes or formats for volunteer management" to improve both centralized control and oversight. The first change under this proposal was to appoint a volunteer manager who would oversee all changes and operations of volunteers. This appointment was the sole new position created. However, the plan also called for the identification and appointment of Staff Volunteer Liaisons in Community Libraries and in all relevant work departments. In other words, within this very large system, named persons were assigned the job of furthering the up-and-down communication between administration and library work units. In addition, the plan called for "standardizing forms and procedures, so the basis of communication is understood" by all supervisors, staff, and volunteers. For smaller libraries, it is important to have someone in charge of volunteers, even if it is only part of the person's work assignment. In any department that uses volunteers, a staff member should be designated to ensure that the volunteer program is working well.

Communication

The plan called for improvements in internal communication about volunteers in order to "determine [the] best way for staff and administrative decision makers to share information on an ongoing basis." The plan noted that KCLS was "automating all volunteer management processes with software that empowers volunteers to apply online, view their schedules, and enter or review their volunteer hours. The software helps staff be more efficient with routine volunteer processes, giving them increased time to plan and provide services."

This process included the standardization of volunteer forms and procedures, so the basis of communication would be understood within the system. Its external component was a branding program that helped all volunteers to be clearly identified and would serve to market the program to the public. And last in the communication changes, the writers called for automating all volunteer management processes with software that empowered volunteers to apply online, view their schedules, and enter or review their volunteer hours. The software helps staff be more efficient with routine volunteer processes, giving them increased time to plan and provide services. (See Chapter 8 for the planning and the result of installing this electronic information system at KCLS.) Smaller libraries may not need to elaborate such formal communication lines, but every volunteer program needs to keep track of who, what, and when of the program. Principals, library directors, and boards also need to get clear communication about library volunteers to assure that everybody is clear on how the program works—and whether or not it is achieving its expected results as stated in the institution's annual plan and/or long-term strategic plan.

Recruitment

The new manager of volunteers and other designated administrators were given the responsibility for determining the best methods to identify potential volunteers, recruit them to the organization, and select the ones they wanted. Because KCLS had become so thoroughly wedded to electronic communication for both internal and external messages, it was natural for the plan to recommend new web pages on the KCLS site geared specifically to volunteer recruitment. As part of establishing the volunteer recruitment program, the planners called for system-wide volunteer recognition events. Since the authors of this volume agree with this integrated approach, they have treated recognition as part of the recruitment and retention processes covered in Chapter 6.

Training

The purpose of KCLS training was to make volunteers effective. Already operating an extensive training program, this bullet was not detailed. The assumption was that the volunteer recruitment would be assumed by the various units within the system that handled training.

At the same time, the administration and board stated a significant caveat: The Friends of KCLS volunteer program was outside the scope of the planning committee working to improve volunteers. The "Friends," the planning team noted, were quite distinctive. KCLS encouraged the formation of Friends of the Library groups in the communities where its branches were located. In 2008, 36 Friends groups raised funds to support special projects and activities at the branch or work unit level. In 2005, the library raised more than $250,000 in support of special programs and activities throughout the library system.[3]

A VOLUNTEER PROGRAM MISSION STATEMENT: WHAT SHOULD IT SAY AND WHY?

As part of self-conscious management, your library may decide that it wants to create a mission statement for the volunteer program. If you do, the KCLS Volunteer Program Mission Statement is a good model from which to build your own. Here is the statement and our analysis of it.

Example: King County (WA) Library System Volunteer Program Mission Statement.[4]

King County Library System welcomes and encourages volunteers. Volunteers enrich the capabilities of the Library System. Volunteers may donate their time in the community libraries or on system-wide special projects and events. Volunteer service is performed with guidance and support from the King County Library System.

This mission statement came into existence during the reorganization of the volunteer program in 2008. The intent of the mission statement was to reflect the history and changes that would be made in the library's volunteer program.

The first sentence of the mission sets the tone: KCLS "welcomes and encourages volunteers." Why? The rationale is stated in sentence two of the mission: Because "volunteers enrich the capabilities of the Library System." The key word is "enrich," which suggests improvement—i.e., the purpose of the volunteer program is to improve the system's services to its constituencies. In other words, changes in the volunteer program will be judged against KCLS's mission and goals.

The third sentence further prescribes the relationship between the library and its volunteers: That is, the "volunteers may donate their time." In other words, volunteering can be done only with the permission of the library system, that is, within the mandates the system specifies. This same sentence exemplifies two different types of volunteering—"within community libraries" or for "system-wide special projects and events."

Finally, the last sentence in the mission statement returns to the authoritative position: "Volunteers may expect both guidance [as in training and oversight] and support [which implicitly includes volunteers in the health and safety provisions that staff workers receive when they work for the library]."

The authors recognize that some libraries may not want separate mission statements for their volunteer program. Even without such a statement, those who are starting a new or reforming an old volunteer's program need to think hard about the limits of the volunteer program before they start recruiting. Whether or not your organization decides to develop a volunteer program mission statement, its administrators need to find ways to articulate the benefits that the library expects to derive from the use of volunteers and the benefits to volunteers and the service community—*before* recruiting those volunteers.

KCLS HISTORICAL OVERVIEW OF THE VOLUNTEER PROGRAM[5]

Volunteers have always supported the King County Library System by assisting staff in their work to move materials through the system and to serve patrons. Many community members turn to the libraries to help them fulfill community service hours for schools, courts, and other organizations; to help them increase their skills and knowledge; or simply to help them find a place where they can serve others. Volunteering is a partnership with library staff to sustain and expand the system's reach.

By 2008, volunteer services at KCLS were largely decentralized, with each of the libraries recruiting and managing volunteers separately and using a variety of homegrown forms and procedures. Additionally, several effective service programs were managed centrally, but provided in the libraries. These programs are Study Zone, which provides volunteer homework tutors; NetMasters, providing computer classes for patrons in the libraries; Talk Time and Citizenship, which support the library's literacy services through volunteer class facilitators; and Outreach, which coordinates volunteers who bring library materials to less mobile patrons.

The Volunteer Coordination Project began in the summer of 2008 as a direct result of KCLS staff members voicing concerns and raising questions of the use and support of volunteers. In response, KCLS administration, through the Employee Involvement Project, created a project charter with responsibility to recommend methods to streamline and enhance the coordination, management, and recruitment of KCLS volunteers. The committee's recommendations began to be implemented in July 2009.

ANALYSIS BASED ON RESEARCH OF THE VOLUNTEER COORDINATION PROJECT COMMITTEE

The KCLS Administrative Planning Team began its report on their planning for the future of volunteers by stating a clear premise about the program. Volunteerism is recognized as helpful to the core work of providing "outstanding library service."

KCLS administration supports the valuable relationship we have with our volunteers. The program improvements provide a foundation from which the volunteer program can become more innovative and relevant to the needs of current and future volunteers, as KCLS continues its tradition of outstanding library service.[6]

Here is a summary of the issues with which the KCLS Administrative Planning Team had to deal in order to improve its volunteer program:

The Volunteer Coordination Project (VCP) began in the summer of 2008 as a direct result of KCLS staff members voicing concerns and raising questions of the use and support of volunteers. In response to these concerns, KCLS administration, through the Employee Involvement Project, created a project charter with responsibility to recommend methods that streamline and enhance the coordination, management, and recruitment of KCLS volunteers.

Specific objectives include:

- Recommend consistent processes or formats for volunteer management.
- Identify best practices for recruiting and selecting volunteers.
- Determine best way for staff to share information.
- Explore training needs for staff and volunteers.
- Ongoing communication with KCLS staff and decision makers.

The Friends of KCLS volunteer program is outside the scope of this committee and not considered in the report. The Volunteer Coordination Project Team gathered input and information both internally and externally. Internally, the VCP Team:

- Administered a comprehensive staff survey to over 200 staff members.
- Solicited input from a sampling of current volunteers.
- Received direct input from staff.
- Engaged cluster management teams for input and volunteer data.
- Investigated the flow of information and statistical data for staff and volunteers.

Externally, the VCP Team:

- Reviewed and gathered volunteer management and library-based volunteer program literature and resources.
- Researched other comparable public libraries and their volunteer management systems.

The above input resulted in the identification of the following broad issues: Support, Expectations, Formalization, Communication, and Benefits. While the volunteer program at KCLS accomplishes a great deal and a general positive feeling exists by staff and volunteers, some problems are evident. These include staff not certain of:

- What procedures to follow
- Who to turn to for support
- Which volunteer duties are permissible

Furthermore, some staff regard volunteers as taking away paid hours and employees' duties.

Volunteers reflect their satisfaction of giving back to their community and contributing to an institution they value and, at the same time, express the following concerns:

- Lack of appreciation
- Isolation
- Occasional feeling of resentment by staff

Information flow is not always clear, tools and procedures vary widely, and success is not celebrated consistently and to the fullest extent.

To build on the strengths of this broad program and to address the problems listed above, the following recommendations focus on:

- Staffing
- Internal culture
- Staff tools
- Volunteer experience[7]

The preceding analysis recognizes two important points in particular. First, the recommendations for changes in the volunteer program are not going to involve changes in the Friends of the King County Library System. (A section on Friends groups is found in Chapter 7.) The second point is that the report is straightforward in suggesting that isolation and lack of information are weaknesses of the way that the volunteer program was currently being operated. If you are a reader working in a smaller library, you might be tempted to think that feelings of isolation are a function of KCLS's large size. That is not the case, however. Poor communication—not size—is the most significant reason for why staff feel isolated. As any divorce lawyer can tell you, feelings of isolation can be found in the most intimate circumstance in which two persons are involved. To help break down this isolation, KCLS researchers recommended and implemented several recommendations and staff changes to make sure that workforce communication changes were made for the better.

RECOMMENDATIONS FOR CHANGES IN THE VOLUNTEER PROGRAM[8]

Staff Changes

Identify a central point person to oversee KCLS volunteer activities. A central staff member committed to the operations of the volunteers at KCLS will be invaluable for coordinating, promoting, and supporting this program and managing the tools, training, visibility, and accountability recommended below.

Designate a Volunteer Liaison with a planned training schedule. Currently, this position is optional, informal, and unconnected to their peers. A more structured network will improve central information dissemination.

Reduce staff concerns and questions and create a means for staff members to support each other. Twice-yearly trainings are recommended for this group, with focus on recognition, statistics reporting, recruiting, and retention.

Create a Volunteer Advisory Committee. As a support and task base for the central point person, such a committee can bring in diverse ideas, help create trainings and engage a core of staff members.

Internal Culture

Develop a Volunteer Mission Statement. Such an effort would help to guide a sustainable volunteer program and reflect a top level commitment to volunteer support.

Create an internal marketing campaign. Strong staff survey responses reflect confusion, concern, and an inconsistent understanding of policies, permissible tasks, procedures, and reporting of volunteer activities.

Increase visibility of branch volunteers. System programs such as Study Zone and Words on Wheels benefit from centrally coordinated efforts to support that volunteer corps. In an effort to strengthen the volunteer program as a whole and create parity amongst all volunteers, branch volunteers will benefit from greater central support.

Staff Tools

Create a Volunteer Wiki for staff. KCLS staff members have increased facility with web-based tools and would benefit from a single, dedicated space to share volunteer best practices and learn from each other. Such a tool can also conveniently host policies, procedures, and resources to support staff and be readily updated.

Create system-wide standards. Staff has indicated a perception of a lack of standards and clarity for the following issues: court-ordered volunteers, age limits, letters of reference, and separation process.

Standardize Intake Forms. With four different system-level volunteer programs and 43 library volunteer opportunities, KCLS lacks a consistent set of information for volunteers. This leads to the possibility of incomplete information, duplication of effort for staff supervising volunteers who move within the system, and a missed opportunity to accurately track hours and recognize milestones consistently.

Write Volunteer Job Descriptions. A barrier for employing volunteers at a library is the effort needed to create meaningful work. Providing a menu of basic job descriptions and/or a template for permissible volunteer jobs would facilitate staff efforts to train and support library volunteers.

Improve Statistic Reporting. Current volunteer statistic reporting is inconsistent, incomplete, and/or duplicative throughout KCLS. A comprehensive approach is needed to ensure that all volunteer hours are recorded and that the Business Office and KCLS Board have an accurate count of the effort and benefit that volunteers provide.

Volunteer Experience

Promote and align public web content. A consistent look and format for all volunteer-related pages would reflect a comprehensive approach; visibility on the home page would improve volunteer access.

Improve recognition efforts. Staff indicates a desire for more ideas, support and tangible rewards for recognizing volunteers; volunteers express a deep appreciation of acknowledgment they receive for their activities.

Enrich the daily volunteer experience. Volunteers express that they are motivated by an enriched experience yet also indicate inconsistent support and interactions among themselves and with library staff. Secure space for volunteers while performing their tasks is also desired. A systematic approach of site orientation, recognition, and enrichment activities will help to fully engage and fulfill KCLS volunteers. Furthermore, a regular schedule of surveying of all volunteers will provide KCLS with needed data to support the needs and meet the expectations of this generous group.

Smaller libraries may have simpler procedures, but it is important for programs of any size to manage staff, record keeping and the volunteer's experience.

BUILDING ADMINISTRATIVE CAPACITY:
VOLUNTEER PROJECT COORDINATOR

The description that follows was used to hire a new volunteer coordinator at King County (Washington) Library System in preparation for reforming its volunteer program in 2008–2009. This description has been vetted by a large library administration and by legal counsel for that library. Note how the position has been placed in the administrative hierarchy as a person reporting directly to the director of community relations, who in turn reports to the director of the library. To sum up, the volunteer project coordinator is given wide authority as a KCLS operating officer with a reporting line that leads almost immediately to the organization's executive director.

This volunteer coordinator's description aptly illustrates how to deal with multiple issues in the establishment or management of a volunteer program. A volunteer director's problems typically begin when the job description grants too much autonomy or provides insufficient autonomy to the person holding this position. Even if yours is a small library, your position description of the director of volunteers needs to demonstrate integration into the library administrative and work landscape. That's because the effective director of a volunteer program handles many issues that cross work unit boundaries and involve external as well as internal relations of the library.

Keep these stiff work requirements in mind. This is the last place you want to appoint someone whose principal (or only) qualification is to be "a nice person," someone "who likes to work with people." Those elements are necessary, but so is being savvy (and hopefully being able to demonstrate experience in handling how organizations function, the adaptability that matches how library work often is accomplished, and how partnership organizations function.)

Note that the volunteer manager described here is in the authority lines of the Community Relations Department. This placement is logical because the greatest advantage of the volunteer program is external. The appointment in this direction says that volunteers are not staff, and they cannot and should not be treated like staff. What the volunteers will do may be needed to ease particular staff situations, but volunteers should be managed as resources that principally help to market the institution.

Another nice feature of this job description is that it builds flexibility into the position. The work outline suggests that authority and tasks will vary according to circumstances and to the directions that the institution wants to go. One year and one administrator may take volunteers in one direction. Another year and another director may take it in a different direction.

Concluding this introduction, remember that one of the most difficult and least discussed aspects of volunteer program coordination is how much time it takes to breed and hold quality to standards into various volunteer programs. The natural tendency of newcomer board members and pressures from outside organizations can make a shambles out of continuity, especially standards set up as quality benchmarks.

Title: Volunteer Project Coordinator[9]
Department: Community Relations
Reports to: Director, Community Relations
Effective: Date: July 1, 2009
General Assignment Summary:

Oversee and coordinate the implementation of appropriate Volunteer Coordination Project (VCP) recommendations through the development of a comprehensive Plan, which broadly include streamlining and enhancing the coordination, management, recruitment and recognition of all KCLS volunteers;

Perform a variety of administrative, analytical, training and technical tasks related to this effort; support the work of the Volunteer liaisons (to be created); oversee the interface with other necessary KCLS departments to successfully manage the effort (HR, Business Office, ITS, Outreach, Community Relations/Graphics and Public Services);

Consult and/or foster partnerships with outside volunteer organizations/agencies to more broadly promote and recruit KCLS volunteers.

The first task of the volunteer manager is to implement the planning recommendations that come from administration. This mandate suggests the "baggage" that the new administrator will carry. The first job is to continue the planning process, to coordinate and streamline the work that already has been done. In other words, the volunteer coordinator is about both continuity and change.

The second role sets the authority of the coordinator. The appointed person is not a manager at the highest level and not independently ranked within the organization. The volunteer coordinator reports to a knowledgeable administrator who already understands the balance that the organization is attempting to accomplish. The appointment creates a functional position to work with other intermediate managers to make volunteers work—through the higher-level administration and to represent the higher administrator as an administrative minion.

The third assignment is external. The need is for someone who will "foster partnerships" with other organizations as an appointed representative of the administration.

Essential Duties/Major Responsibilities:

Any of the following duties may be performed. These examples are not necessarily performed by all incumbents, however, and do not include all specific tasks an incumbent may be expected to perform.

1. Manage projects, develop and implement plans as necessary for the successful implementation of KCLS' volunteer program and manage committees and teams related to the effort.

2. Evaluate processes, operations, activities and policies and procedures related to volunteers; recommend improvements and modifications; write and update communications, collect and analyze data and prepare various reports.
3. Generate staff understanding and participation within the Volunteer Coordination Plan and structure.
4. Develop and recommend improvements to the Volunteer Coordination Plan as implementation proceeds.
5. Plan, coordinate and participate with the Staff Training department to offer staff volunteer coordination and motivation development opportunities.
6. Collect relevant data/information as requested.
7. Assure compliance with Library policy, Human Resource, Business Department, ITS and Community Relations requirement.

Item 7, immediately above, articulates the importance of compliance with all institutional policies in regard to volunteers. Library managers should treat volunteers with the same respect and expectations as staff. That includes procedural steps in removal, especially if the volunteer is engaged in some controversial area that in any way could be deemed whistle-blowing. In short, you can't get rid of a volunteer simply because they have told someone that the library where they volunteer is "doing bad stuff" involving the library's procedures in accounting, internal controls, auditing, labor and employment or environmental matters. To quote from one section of Federal law, "A whistleblower policy encourages staff and volunteers to come forward with credible information on illegal practices or violations of adopted policies of the organization, specifies that the organization will protect the individual from retaliation, and identifies those staff or board members or outside parties to whom such information can be reported."[10]

BUILDING ADMINISTRATIVE CAPACITY: CLUSTER VOLUNTEER SERVICES LIAISON

Many library directors make a fetish out of how few administrators it takes to operate their library with its levels of budget expenditure and number of staff. What often occurs when you analyze these administration-short organizations is how much their operations are based on "everybody doing their jobs" without much sense of "what really needs to get done," or in checking to see if those jobs get done—and that they are accomplished at a high level of service quality.

"Great administration" far too often is recognized externally as those who spend a lot of time away from their office seeking and getting public acclaim for their work outside their organization. That often is the antithesis of effective organizational management—which can be defined as quality services and products delivered on a regular and efficient basis and in such a way as to have measurable impact in the service consistency.

The KCPL Volunteer Coordination Project Committee recognizes the complexity of obtaining volunteer effectiveness within the organization by giving the enriched volunteer program both an enhanced executive capacity (i.e., the volunteer services coordinator) and operational depth and breadth through the creation of a cluster volunteer services functional liaison

There are two points worth noting about this new position. First, its awkward name matched the way KCLS had arrayed its services—i.e., in clusters. The job of this particular individual is clearly identified in the use of the term "functional liaison" as serving like a principal operating officer within each cluster of branches. The important work that this person would do, the committee asserted, would be to make the volunteer system function by making sure that communication about volunteers takes place through the whole organization.

Note also that this liaison reports to the library cluster manager and not to the volunteer services coordinator. Notice how this authority line and communications responsibilities are arrayed in this job description. This statement clearly says that the first responsibility of this position is to help the cluster volunteers be successful and to represent the cluster's volunteer interests with the central administration. Moreover, the job description articulates the need to protect the legal status of both volunteers and library workers. Volunteering in a library of any size involves legal responsibilities for the library and its employees.

Smaller libraries might not need this middle management position, but the tasks of making sure volunteers receive consistent, high-quality supervision on a day-to-day basis needs to be planned for.

Title: Cluster Volunteer Services Liaison[11]
Department: Library Cluster
Reports to: Director, Cluster Services Manager
Effective Date: July 1, 2009

General Assignment Summary

The Volunteer Services Liaison reports to the Library Cluster manager and cluster management team and is responsible for supporting strong working relationships between the cluster's staff and volunteers. The liaison does this by ensuring awareness, and understanding of KCLS volunteer policies, guidelines, procedures, tools, issues and opportunities in order to clarify expectations, limit liability and risk, and provide consistently outstanding volunteer experiences.

The liaison may also supervise volunteers. If so, this person will interact with the variety of volunteers who participate in KCLS volunteer programs, such as Study Zone and NetMaster, as well as those who perform library-specific tasks. These volunteers may be teens, adults, college students, seniors, and people with ability challenges.

The Liaison will maintain routine communication and coordination with the KCLS Volunteer Services Coordinator [or similarly assigned position], his/her peers in the same liaison role, the cluster Community Liaison, Public Services, the System volunteer program coordinators (Study Zone, NetMasters, Talk Time, Words on Wheels), the Business Office, and KCLS Community Relations, to enable timely responses to staff and volunteer concerns, strategic planning, and effective delivery of library services through volunteers.

The Liaison has regular interaction with branch staff who supervise ... volunteers and serves in an oversight capacity to direct their work as it relates to recruiting, selecting, supervising, coaching, and recognizing volunteers.

The liaison may also supervise volunteers. If so, this person will interact with the variety of volunteers who participate in KCLS volunteer programs, such as Study Zone and NetMaster, as well as those who perform library-specific tasks. These volunteers may be teens, adults, college students, seniors, and people with ability challenges.

The Liaison will maintain routine communication and coordination with the KCLS Volunteer Services Coordinator [or similarly assigned position], his/her peers in the same liaison role, the cluster Community Liaison, Public Services, the System volunteer program coordinators (Study Zone, NetMasters, Talk Time, Words on Wheels), the Business Office, and KCLS Community Relations, to enable timely responses to staff and volunteer concerns, strategic planning, and effective delivery of library services through volunteers.

Essential Duties /Major Responsibilities

- Acts as the point of contact for the KCLS Volunteer Services Coordinator to disseminate volunteer -related communication and participate as needed in an advisory capacity, communicating the needs of library volunteers and staff.
- Maintains contact with other volunteer program coordinators (Study Zone, NetMaster, etc) as needed to help implement and coordinate these programs in the cluster's libraries.
- Sustains staff buy-in for the value of volunteers by encouraging a positive and welcoming environment for volunteers.
- Provides assistance and leadership for volunteer appreciation.
- Ensures implementation by cluster staff of all volunteer-related policy, guideline, or procedural updates.
- May help train volunteers or hold volunteer orientation sessions.
- Assists with any conflicts that may arise in supervision or utilization of volunteers in the libraries.
- Ensures that those who supervise volunteers maintain current records and required documents and report accurate statistics.
- Implements record keeping software provided by KCLS to track volunteer statistics by individual library and creates reports as requested.
- May present stories and positive communication to APT [the Administrative Planning Team], the KCLS Trustees, or other governing bodies that effectively recognize and share the success of KCLS volunteers.

Essential Skills

- Clearly and succinctly communicates ideas both verbally and in writing
- Strong interpersonal communication skills
- Solid problem-solving skills
- Ability to build long-term internal and external loyalty and relationships

- Initiative, creativity and resourcefulness
- Uses discretion, diplomacy, and tact in dealing with volunteers
- Makes sound decisions based on in-depth knowledge of KCLS priorities, projects, and plans
- Strong presentation and facilitation skills
- Experience and sensitivity working with gender, ethnic/culturally diverse groups

VOLUNTEER SERVICES POLICY (VSP)[12]

The VSP is inserted in the management policies book of the KCLS. The policy begins by stating that its words serve as the foundation for the VMP. And, its main purpose is to make sure that the staff recognize and understand its various aspects so they can implement the objects of the policy. The beginning and the end of volunteer policy, then, is its placement as a legitimate feature of the library's policy-driven operations.

Volunteer time, energy and goodwill are invaluable assets to the King County Library System (KCLS). Volunteerism enhances KCLS' ability to fulfill its mission by providing opportunities for direct public participation in community libraries. This policy serves as the foundation for KCLS' volunteer management program, which guides and empowers staff to effectively recruit, manage, communicate with, support and recognize all volunteers.

Statement of Policy

The work performed by volunteers shall not result in a loss of authorized hours for employees (Agreement By and Between KCLS and Washington State Council of County and City Employees AFSCME AFL-CIO, Local 1857, *Article 26.1*). Volunteers may assist paid KCLS staff with their regular tasks, as tong as they do not perform all of the tasks of a regular position during their volunteer day and therefore act as an unpaid staff member. If the library does not have specific work available for an interested person, staff should not create new work or divide up work performed by another volunteer.

This specific admonition concerns the library's agreement with its major union. The policy stipulates that volunteer work may supplement the regular work of a staff member, but it may not replace that paid work in any way. As we suggested earlier in this book, this issue of volunteers as replacement workers ought to be handled in advance of attempting to set up a high-visibility, positive volunteer program.

When volunteer labor is intended to replace paid work, especially the labor of paid librarians and those technical specialists who are integral to the performance of these professional duties, then that issue ought to be clearly stated. The announcement that volunteer labor will be used to operate a library so that it doesn't close is incredibly demeaning to libraries generally and to library professionals specifically. It is a sad instance when civic and elected officials make such a claim.

Next, there is a statement of specific activities that, under no circumstance, volunteers should perform.

No Volunteer Can:

- Perform activities that could reveal confidential patron information
- Use the Integrated Library System (ILS)
- Handle Library System money
- Perform volunteer tasks outside library premises, except in "virtual" and outreach assignments

The first of these is a prohibition against handling patron information, which in many states would breech the confidentiality law that protects library user information, a law that until recent federal legislation was respected by most law enforcement agencies.

The second prohibition, like the first, involves access to patron data—and to collections data as well. In an ILS, it is usually a relatively easy task to move from the patron data module to the collections module. Most volunteers can be trusted, but a library would not be smart to put the ability to steal collections or have access to patron data in the theft opportunity network of a nonpaid employee trained in the rules of confidentiality.

The third admonition involves library funds, including handling donations and counter charges for materials and fines.

The fourth admonition is a bit hazier in the case of most library systems. Many libraries have volunteer storytellers and volunteer speaker's bureaus. This prohibition obviously had a specific instance behind it, but it might have been more helpful if the specificity was stated.

Affirmative Action Recruitment Pledge

The next paragraph of the policy is the antidiscrimination statement of Federal Law restated in language that fits into this library's policy. It has to be so stated, and all volunteer policies and most public documents ought to have the same statement in one form or another.

Volunteers shall be recruited without regard to any individual's race, creed, color, national origin, religion, marital status, sexual orientation, gender, or any other legally protected characteristic.

Criminal History Check

Under Washington Law, KCLS must obtain a written disclosure from anyone volunteering to work in a position that may involve unsupervised access to children 16 years of age or younger, developmentally disabled persons, or vulnerable adults (see Applicant Disclosure Form). In conjunction with this law, KCLS conducts a Washington State Patrol criminal history check on all volunteer candidates.

This KCLS policy is a clear warning that all volunteers will have a criminal information check run before the library allows them to fill volunteer posts. The language of this paragraph is particularly nuanced as a protection against pedophilia, but since hardly any library position does not involve one of the three groups of at-risk children or adults that are stated in this paragraph, the language gives a fair warning that you will be checked if you attempt to volunteer.

Intriguingly, this particular paragraph has come to be recognized in several different publications as stopping the attempt of seniors to take voluntary slots because they do not believe that anyone has a right to check their credentials like that. Unfortunately, that is not the case, and at least some seniors may see this as a deterrent. On the other hand, it probably also deters those seeking to volunteer who have criminal records.

Minors as Volunteers

Volunteers under the age of 18 must have parental approval and cannot work more than four hours per day. Volunteers under ... age 14 may not work without direct supervision by a staff member or an adult who has successfully completed the volunteer application process

Another useful feature of a library volunteer policy is one that deals with children under the age of 18, and in this case, an additional provision affecting children under 14. The first sentence designates the need for written parental approval—plus a limit on time worked. The second sentence provides for de facto close supervision of younger children's work.

In our visits to many libraries, we have found some of them extraordinarily sloppy in their use of children as volunteers. In King County no librarian has a right to accept a 14- or a 17-year-old volunteer into a volunteer situation without clearing that person with the appropriate supervisory offices in the library system.

Some librarians probably will hoot at this requirement since they have been handling it in a more personal way in their system. However, keep in mind that a library's liability and insurance systems both come into play when any volunteer is chosen to work in or for a library system. Library administrations would do well to explain the concept of contingent liability to staff who make personnel decisions without checking with staff who are specialists in this field of administration.

Another kind of volunteer that needs special attention is the type who needs the attention that can only be given in a sheltered workshop situation. We have had excellent work with mentally retarded and developmentally disabled (MRDD) juveniles and adults in putting out mailings, in simple sorting tasks, etc. The supervision of these persons needs to be tighter, too, to protect these vulnerable souls from harm while they are in your workplace; and to make sure that work is properly assigned and supervised to minimize errors. Closer supervision also should include friendly and caring help to learn while working.

Court-Ordered Volunteers

KCLS will attempt to accommodate volunteer candidates seeking to fulfill a requirement for court-ordered community service. In addition to the criteria in the Volunteer Services Guidelines, court-ordered volunteers must be willing to disclose the nature of their offense on the Volunteer Application forms and successfully clear the criminal history check.

Most court-ordered volunteers are not violent and simply have traffic violations. Of course, there are exceptions. The most profound example of this requirement was when one of the authors of this book discovered that one of its library volunteers had murdered her husband some 20 years earlier. Admittedly, the husband had been violently abusive, but there was a staff discussion that took place on how the situation should be handled if some of our "nice women volunteers" discovered that they were working with a volunteer with a murder in her background. Would they have been amused, chagrined, or celebratory?

Court-ordered volunteers can be an enormous help to libraries that need various kinds of assistance. Many of them like tasks that involve physical labor, food, and the attention of a responsible supervisor who knows how to handle workers in a respectful manner.

Close supervision is a must, not to keep crimes from being committed, but to ensure that no one can make such accusations without a paid staff member being able to step forward to point out that she or he was supervising the person or persons for the whole time when a purse or some DVDs had been stolen.

Expectations of Volunteers

Volunteers are expected to conduct themselves as a representative of KCLS and must adhere to the terms of the Volunteer Agreement. Volunteers can be released from volunteer duties at any time.

References

KCLS does not hold volunteers to strict standards for performance. For that reason, volunteer supervisors may not provide references regarding the quality of work performed by a volunteer.

For employment, college or scholarships applications, a volunteer's supervisor may verify the dates and hours worked by a volunteer, as well as a description of the volunteer's tasks, using KCLS' Volunteer Reference Letter Template.

For many volunteers, this limitation on volunteer recommendations in the previous two paragraphs is significant, because many volunteers choose to work without pay to build a resume, hoping for a solid recommendation from a volunteer work supervisor even though no salary was involved. KCLS has very good reasons for why it refuses to get into the "recommendation business" for its volunteers as it takes too much staff time and may have legal implications.

Other libraries may want to handle this matter differently. Some libraries take a different tack: Bethlehem Public Library in Delmar, New York, for example, builds the opportunity for young teens to obtain a "first job recommendation" from their library volunteer experience.[13] No matter how you handle it, however, this issue needs to be addressed by those who make your library's policies and by those who provide orientation and training to your new volunteers.

VOLUNTEER SERVICES GUIDELINES[14]

The Volunteer Services Guideline is intended to guide staff as they encounter and make use of volunteers. The guidelines are procedural and refer staff to other documents for more specialized knowledge. The main intent of the guidelines is to serve as a checklist, so that staff do not forget an important requirement in the selection and supervision of the volunteer. Note the reasons for the guidelines are to make planning and decisions easier while limiting risk and liability.

Date of Origin: 4/10
Procedure Owner(s): Director of *Community Relations and Marketing*
Approved By: Public Services Team
Purpose

In order to provide consistently outstanding volunteer experiences, the King County Library System (KCLS) has developed the following guidelines to be used by staff in conjunction with KCLS' Volunteer Services Policy. These guidelines facilitate planning and decisions related to volunteers while limiting liability and risk.

GUIDELINES

To aid in welcoming interest in volunteering, staff should be familiar with the following guidelines:

Recruitment

Potential volunteers are recruited through in-person inquiries, online or through special recruitment campaigns. KCLS does not accept walk-in volunteers. All volunteers must complete the Volunteer Application form (including a criminal history check) and submit it to the designated staff member

Selection

Volunteer candidates are accepted at the discretion of the local library staff or program coordinator. Libraries do not have to accept every interested person, but staff should make every attempt to match a person with a volunteer position.

Potential volunteers are evaluated based on any of the following criteria:

- Library need
- Skills of the individual
- Degree of staff time required assisting, training, and supervising the individual
- Staff available to work with the individual

If the library does not have specific work available, candidates may be referred to the United Way of King County **or** Volunteer Match.

The last point in this section provides a guideline for when the KCLS has no position available for the person seeking to volunteer. United Way maintains the list of positions for the whole service area and the metropolitan area surrounding it and Volunteer Match has the same kind of help for the region, the nation and internationally.

Supervision and Scheduling

There is nothing that limits who may supervise volunteers; however, staff designated to serve as a volunteer's supervisor should be notified in advance when they will be expected to do so. Adult volunteers who have successfully completed the volunteer application process (including the criminal history check) may be assigned to supervise minors who are volunteering in the library.

Note the stipulation here that an adult volunteer may supervise minors who are library volunteers.

Individuals supervising a volunteer(s) should:

- Work with the volunteer to establish a mutually agreeable schedule
- Ensure the volunteer knows who is serving as their supervisor for any given shift
- Clearly communicate regarding access and restrictions to the facility and its amenities

These expectations should be documented in the Volunteer Agreement and signed by the volunteer prior to starting work.

Hours and Record Keeping

KCLS encourages volunteers to commit to a minimum number of hours and service length, depending on their program or task description. As long as a volunteer knows his/her specific assignment and is supervised appropriately, the work hours depend on the tasks to be accomplished.

Volunteer supervisors should ensure that every volunteer record all hours worked. Each volunteer must complete their timesheet(s) for each month worked. Volunteer supervisors must then submit the timesheets to the Business Office by the fifth of each month.

To reiterate the major points in this section, this guideline asserts the needs for record keeping and transmission of the record of hours worked as a volunteer to the Business Office, which summarizes the activities of volunteers in the same way that it does the hours of paid staff members. You don't have to use a "Business Office" to track volunteer activity, but you should tabulate your volunteer work hours. They often contain useful planning and marketing information.

Recognition

Community Relations will provide resources to help staff thank volunteers, such as giveaways and note cards, multi-media presentations spotlighting volunteers, and local and System recognition events.

Oversight and Communication

- *Volunteer Services Coordinator (central)*: Oversees KCLS' volunteer program, coordinating and supporting recruitment, selection processes, forms/tools, training, tracking of statistics and volunteer recognition. Communicates directly with Cluster Volunteer Liaisons and System volunteer program coordinators (e.g. Study Zone, Netmasters, Talk Time and Citizenship).

- *Cluster Volunteer Liaison (local)*: Relays information and serves as the "expert" regarding volunteer policies, procedures, guidelines, tasks, tools, issues and opportunities. Communicates directly with Volunteer Services Coordinator.
- *Volunteer Supervisor (local)*: Individual(s) in each library designated to serve as a supervisor to one or more volunteers. Communicates directly with Cluster Volunteer Liaison.

VOLUNTEER RECRUITMENT PROCEDURES[15]

Date of Origin: 4/10
Procedure Owner(s): Director of *Community Relations and Marketing*
Approved By: Public Services Team

The King County Library System (KCLS) welcomes and encourages library volunteers to help KCLS staff meet patron needs in a variety of ways. These procedures describe the standard recruitment, application and selection process for library volunteers managed by library staff.

The last paragraph suggests that sufficient information is contained in this procedure to ensure that any staff member who talks to a volunteer can speak in a complete and authoritative way about how the application and selection procedure works.

The next paragraph lays out procedures as guidelines for staff information flows regarding the need for volunteer positions. A volunteer position begins like most staff positions—with sufficient information from the work unit to ensure to make a case for the addition of volunteers to the workforce. The submission has to contain an estimate of the skills needed and the time the volunteer project will take, plus the nature of the reporting line for the position.

Procedures

To ensure that library volunteers are recruited, screened and selected in a consistent manner, library staff should follow the procedures below:
Submitting an Online Volunteer Listing
After determining that there is a need for volunteer(s) at a location(s), staff must email the following information to volunteer@kcls.org:

1. A description of the volunteer opportunity
2. The targeted volunteer demographic and other descriptions

3. Required or desired skills set or previous training
4. The timeframe (specific start/end dates) or duration of the opportunity
5. The email and phone number for the appropriate library contact person
6. How long to post the volunteer listing

The Volunteer Services Coordinator will receive the information above and will arrange to have the volunteer opportunity posted online within 48 hours. To repost the opportunity or post it at an additional library location, email the Volunteer Services Coordinator directly at *volunteer@kcls.org*.

The staff who submits online volunteer listings must regularly review their posted opportunities and notify the Volunteer Services Coordinator when listing(s) need to be updated, canceled or reposted.

The preceding paragraph creates a warning that staff of the work unit where the volunteer activity is taking place must update the position and project description before recruitment can begin. This information, of course, is needed to make sure that work and liability requirements don't create an untenable situation for a volunteer in a work unit.

Individuals interested in applying for a particular online volunteer listing may contact the library contact person by clicking the "I *am interested in this opportunity*" button within the posting to request a copy of the Volunteer Application form.

The form named in the previous paragraph follows this material on recruitment.

When individuals contact the library and ask how to volunteer, staff should tell them about the online volunteer listing(s), show them how to navigate the volunteer pages on the KCLS Web site (if possible), and explain how to reach the appropriate library contact person. Staff may also print the online volunteer listing and/or the Volunteer Application form for those who are ready to apply.

If an individual cannot find a KCLS volunteer opportunity of interest, staff can show them how to search volunteer listings for other agencies through the United Way of King County or Volunteer Match.

Volunteer Applications

All volunteers must complete the Volunteer Application form. Completed applications should be forwarded to the library contact person designated on the online volunteer listing.

Selection Process

The library contact person designated on the online volunteer listing should:

1. Review each Volunteer Application form for completeness, content and other requirements (e.g. number of hours needed, requests for accommodation).
   a. If clarification is needed, or an application contains requirements that cannot be met, staff should contact the applicant to discuss further and/or explain their concerns.
   b. Applicants may be turned down at this point if they do not meet the selection criteria outlined in the Volunteer Services Guidelines.
2. To process a volunteer's application, send the disclosure form and WSP Criminal History Check form directly to Human Resources. Human Resources will notify staff (via email) and applicants (via US mail) of the results of the check. Staff is not required to take further action for applicants that do not clear the criminal history check. Note: Criminal history checks for volunteers are valid for one year from the date of notification.
3. Once notified that an applicant has cleared the criminal history check, staff should make a reasonable attempt to schedule an informational interview or branch orientation for the applicant(s) to discuss the volunteer tasks and proposed schedule.

The previous two paragraphs outline a communications process, answering the implicit question of how the application process will move from one work unit to another. Even in small libraries, this kind of information is necessary so that staff and volunteers can find out in an expeditious way if a particular volunteer position has been opened and their status in bringing the project into the library work environment.

3a. If both parties agree that the volunteer opportunity is a good match, then staff should document, review and complete the KCLS Volunteer Agreement form with the applicant.
3b. If staff decides that an applicant is not a good match for the volunteer opportunity, they should explain to the applicant why they are not being selected (based on the criteria outlined in the Volunteer Services Guidelines).

4. Applicants that are not selected for a given volunteer opportunity should be notified that they were not selected and encouraged to apply for other opportunities in the future or told that they will be placed on the waitlist, if available (see definition below).

5. Once a volunteer has been officially selected staff should note the date the Volunteer Agreement was signed on the Volunteer Application and send a copy of the completed Volunteer Application to the Volunteer Services Coordinator to be documented as an active volunteer. Copies may be sent electronically.

Definitions

- Volunteer: A person who offers to perform a task or service voluntarily without pay.
- Volunteering: The practice of people working on behalf of others or a particular cause without payment for their time and services.
- Waitlists: A process used by library staff for interested volunteers that are not immediately accepted. Staff has the option to keep pre-qualified volunteers on the waitlist for one (1) year, after which the individuals must reapply and complete the criminal history check.

KCLS CURRENT VOLUNTEER PROGRAMS[16]

KCLS Study Zone Tutors Both Online and Virtual are dedicated volunteers who use their skills in math, science, English, social studies, study methods and more to help students, grades K–12, who can "drop in" for homework help any time during Study Zone hours. Study Zone tutors provide help in all subject areas up to the 8th grade level and also specialize in one or two subjects up to the college-prep level. The Study Zone is a great place for students to study, do homework and get help with their questions. Study Zone Tutors function in two settings:

1) *Library Tutors*: Study Zone volunteers assist students *in KCLS community libraries*. The minimum commitment is two hours a week for one semester (September–January, February–June or July–August). Training is provided. Tutors may renew their commitment at the end of each semester.

2) *Online Virtual Tutors*: The Study Zone Online program provides help for students at libraries where live tutors are not available. Online Study Zone volunteers use their personal computer to connect with students through an online classroom. The minimum commitment is three hours a week for one semester (September–January or February–June). Training provided.

KCLS Talk Time Volunteer Facilitators commit to helping people practice their conversational English skills by facilitating one hour and a half session, once per week during the summer (June–August) or year-round; each session may require up to one hour of lesson plan prep time; attend one four-hour training session; and attend one one-hour orientation. All Talk Time volunteers must be 18 years or older.

KCLS Literacy Towards Citizenship Program Volunteers. Citizenship Volunteer facilitators help people study for the U.S Naturalization Test by facilitating one two-hour session, once per week during the summer or year-round. Candidates attend one one-hour orientation. All Citizenship volunteers must be 18 years or older

KCLS Words on Wheels Outreach volunteers deliver library materials to patrons in adult family homes or group homes who cannot easily visit their community libraries. These include people who have difficulty walking, carrying books, seeing titles of books on shelves or are unable to drive and expect to need help for at least four months. Volunteers are responsible for their own transportation. They pick up materials at their community library and take them to their assigned patron(s). All KCLS materials are available through Words on Wheels

KCLS NetMaster Volunteers teach others how to use personal computers and the Internet in KCLS libraries. By training enthusiastic and knowledgeable volunteers to help with computer training, the NetMaster program helps KCLS achieve our goal of providing free and relevant computer instruction to patrons. NetMaster program goals include:

- Providing a consistent curriculum of fundamental information for anyone learning about personal computers and the Internet in a KCLS library.
- Meeting the diverse needs of patrons whose computer skills and knowledge varies widely, with a focus on introductory level skills.
- Allowing scope for each trainer's individual creativity and knowledge.
- Placing the Internet in context as an information source that supplements and extends traditional library resources.

Volunteers should have basic knowledge in the skills they plan to teach, but they don't need to be computer experts. What's most important is attitude: patience, kindness, and the ability to explain computer information in a simple, clear fashion. Net-Masters must be at least 18 years old. Each NetMaster volunteer is asked to teach a minimum of four classes over a period of six months. Many NetMasters teach one class a month, while some teach more. As libraries try to maintain a regular schedule of classes for the public, they tend to prefer someone who teaches on a fairly regular basis. KCLS offers considerable flexibility in scheduling classes. Classes can be taught during weekdays, weekends, and evenings

King County Library System uses several hundred volunteers a year, and at most locations they have waiting lists for people who want to volunteer when a volunteer position opens up. Because of the system's size, the popularity of the volunteer program, and the usefulness of the volunteers, system administrators went to the effort of creating an organized, professionally led program. The above documents and commentary are offered as examples of what other libraries should consider for their volunteer programs. Not every library will chose the same structure as KCLS, but all libraries should consider the issues raised in this case study.

NOTES

1. KCLS, "Volunteer, Define, Align, Empower: Developing a Coordinated Volunteer Program," Supporting Materials for KCLS Presentation at American Library Association Annual Conference June 2011, New Orleans, LA (Issaquah, WA: King County Library System, June 2011).

2. This and other quotes that follow all come from KCLS, "Volunteer," 2.

3. KCLS, "Friends of the Library," At http://www.kcls.org/about/support/volunteers/friends.cfm (accessed January 6, 2013).

4. KCLS, "Volunteer," 2.

5. Ibid., 2.

6. Ibid., 2.

7. Ibid., 3.

8. Ibid., 4.

9. Ibid., 5.

10. National Council of Nonprofits, "Whistleblower Protection Policies," http://www.councilofnonprofits.org/resources/resources-topic/boards-governance/whistleblower-protection-policies (accessed April 12, 2013).

11. KCLS, "Volunteers," 10–11.

12. Ibid., 12–14.

13. Linda Massen, "A Hot Ticket: Middle Schoolers Can't Resist Our Summer Reading Program [Bethlehem Public Library, Delmar, NY]," *School Library Journal*, May 1, 2003, http://www.schoollibraryjournal.com/article/CA294419.html?industryid=47087 (accessed July 5, 2011).

14. KCLS, "Volunteers," 15–17.

15. Ibid., 18–20.

16. Ibid., 6–8.

Index

About the Authors

LESLIE E. HOLT currently consults with libraries, schools, and child-serving agencies. She worked at the St. Louis Public Library as director of Youth Services from June 1990 until 2004. Leslie is a past president of the Association of Library Service for Children (ALSC) and has been active for many years in ALA, PLA, ALSC, and other state and regional library associations. She coauthored *Managing Children's Services in Libraries* (2013) and *Public Library Service to the Poor: Doing All We Can* (2010). She received a BA degree from Cornell College (Iowa), a MA from The University of Chicago in library science, and her PhD from Loyola University of Chicago.

GLEN E. HOLT has been editor of *Public Library Quarterly* since 2004. He was the director of St. Louis Public Library for 17 years. Before that, he operated the Honor's Program in the College of Liberal Arts at the University of Minnesota and taught history and urban studies and chaired the Urban Studies Program at Washington University in St. Louis. Glen led the decade-long research project that resulted in the coauthored *Measuring Your Library's Value: How to Do a Cost-Benefit Analysis for Your Public Library* (2007). He was coauthor of *Library Success: A Celebration of Library Innovation, Adaption and Problem Solving* (2006) and he is coauthor on *Library Services to the Poor: Doing All We Can* (2010), named a winner of PLA's Charlie Robinson Award (2001) for his innovation and risk taking while SLPL's director, and he was one of only a half-dozen U.S. library professionals to be named a "senior networker" for the Bertelsmann Foundation's International Network of Public Librarians from 1998 until 2003. Glen received his BA from Baker University and his master's and doctorate from The University of Chicago.